Va

2·5

A TECH

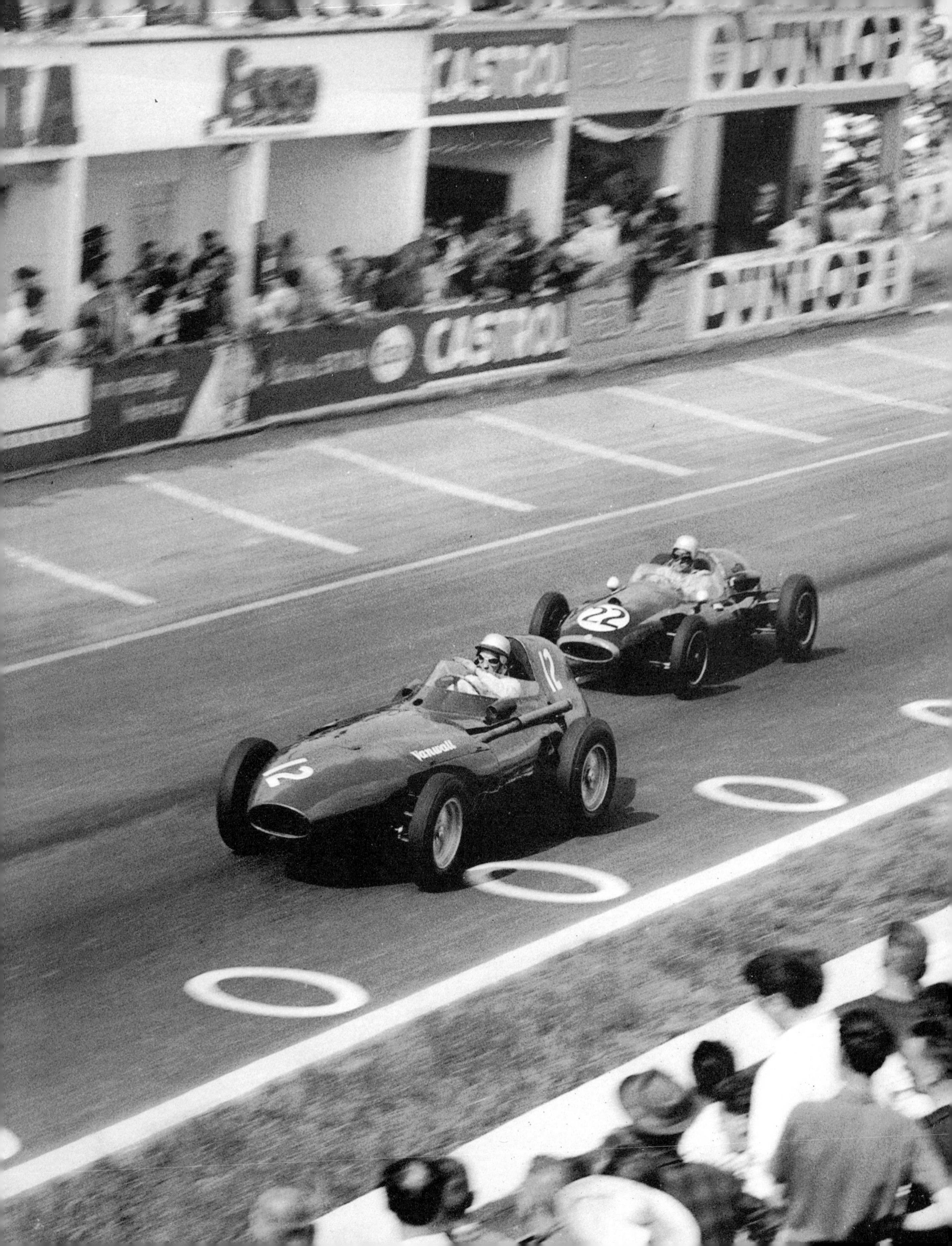
CASTROL
DUNLOP
CASTROL
DUNLOP
Vanwall
12
22

Vanwall
2·5 LITRE F1
A TECHNICAL APPRAISAL

IAN BAMSEY

A **FOULIS** MOTORING BOOK

First published 1990

Published by:
Haynes Publishing Group
Sparkford, Near Yeovil, Somerset BA22 7JJ
England

Haynes Publications Inc.
861 Lawrence Drive, Newbury Park,
California, 91320, USA

Produced for GT Foulis & Co. Ltd. by
RACECAR ENGINEERING
(Racecar Engineering Specialist Publications)
Telephone or Fax (0935) 31295
Editorial Director: Ian Bamsey
Research Assistant: Alan Lis

British Library Cataloguing in Publication Data
Bamsey, Ian
Vanwall - a technical appraisal
1. Racing cars
I. Title
629.22089

ISBN 0-85429-838-X

Library of Congress Catalog
Card number 90-83295

Printed in England by:
J. H. Haynes & Co. Ltd.
Typesetting & Artwork by:
Photosetting, Yeovil, Somerset

INTRODUCTION

Successful Grand Prix cars were red, sometimes silver, never green. At least, it seemed that way in the early Fifties when British patriot Guy Anthony Vandervell started out on his mission to change the colour of things. The owner of a large automotive concern, Vandervell left the BRM project to do things his own way and while BRM continued to flounder the Vanwall team steadily gathered momentum.

The definitive Vanwall arrived in 1956. It had a powerful four cylinder fuel injected engine and an advanced spaceframe, disc braked chassis clothed in an aerodynamic body by Frank Costin. The slippery green machine set a new standard for Grand Prix car streamlining, Costin applying state of the art aerodynamics from the world of aviation.

By 1957 the Vanwall team was up to speed with British hero Stirling Moss leading its challenge to the red cars from the Ferrari and Maserati stables. Appropriately enough the first Grand Prix win came on home soil at Aintree, Moss sharing the honours with compatriot Tony Brooks. Over the latter half of the season Moss won two of the three remaining Grands Prix to emphasise that the Vanwall had come of age.

In 1958 Moss and Brooks won six of nine Grand Prix races to make the Vanwall the World Champion car, though Moss missed the Drivers title by one point. On that note Vandervell disbanded the team, leaving the field clear for the rise of a new generation of tiny mid engined cars - 'fairground specials' as the old guard called them. The Vanwall was the last of the great front engined monsters with the most advanced streamlining.

The author is particularly indebted to Frank Costin for the insight he provided into the complex aerodynamics of the Vanwall. Sadly the late Tony Vandervell did not leave a personal account of the car but the story of his team was well documented by Jenkinson and Posthumas' 1975 book 'Vanwall'.

Additional technical information was culled from various sources while the splendid cutaway drawings are Autocar/ Quadrant Picture Library copyright. All photographs are from the archives of London Art Tech (LAT), Standard House, Bonhill Street, London EC2A 4DA.

BACKGROUND

Seeing Red

Alfa Romeo, Maserati, Ferrari: as Grand Prix racing got underway in the aftermath of World War with a 1.5 litres supercharged, 4.5 litres unsupercharged formula, it did so painted blood red. However, in '49 a 1.5 litre Alta added a splash of green while behind the scenes the much trumpeted BRM was completed.

This was the machine that 350 British companies were backing in an effort to overthrow the red devils. The BRM was the brainchild of ERA Voiturette constructor and star pre-war driver Raymond Mays. Inspired originally to beat Germany's Nazi-supported Grand Prix cars of the Thirties, Mays and ERA partner Peter Berthon - an engineer - had set out seeking support from the British motor industry before the war. The ERA had proved its worth in Voiturette racing but the partners' appeal for a Grand Prix budget had been beaten by the industry switch to armaments...

Before the dust of war settled, Mays, Berthon and Ken Richardson had launched a renewed appeal. In March 1945 Mays argued: "I feel very strongly that the ultimate in any activity is of direct value to the country achieving it. There is no doubt that the motor and associated industries have achieved it in the mechanisation of our forces. It is only fitting that this superiority should be perpetuated as a gesture to the technicians and Servicemen who had made our victory possible - no less than to the masses who have patiently endured so much. It becomes incumbent upon those of us who have the ability to try to produce a car which will securely uphold our place in the very forefront of international competition".

Those sentiments found favour with a number of key individuals in the British motor industry, including Oliver Lucas of Joseph Lucas Ltd, Alfred Owen of the Rubery Owen organisation and Guy Anthony ('Tony') Vandervell of Vandervell Products Ltd. Their powerful companies were prominent among the 350 supporting the British Motor Racing Research Trust, which had been incorporated in July 1947 specifically to back the advanced BRM - British Racing Motors - design of V16 challenger.

Vandervell Products, which the owner had pledged to undertake some of the manufacturing work, was famed for its Thinwall Bearings. The thin wall type of bearing had originated in the USA in the Twenties as a replacement for the earlier thick shell bearing composed entirely of whitemetal. Whitemetal offers first rate bearing properties but its fatigue strength is limited. The thin wall shell bearing consisted of a thin steel backing with a thin whitemetal lining. This composite offered good fatigue strength with the important advantage of greater precision in manufacture allowing easier fitting, thus facilitating maintenance.

Tony Vandervell had learned of thin wall bearings in 1930, while running a small bearing manufacturing company owned by his father, Charles Anthony. Charles had made a fortune in the pioneering days of motoring from auto electrics and had subsequently sold his 'CAV' company to Lucas. In 1932 his son persuaded thin wall co-inventor Ben Hopkins to grant him the licence to serve the UK and Europe, Vandervell Products Ltd being set up the following year. The wealthy father underwrote the costly equipment required, the new form of bearing quickly took off and the war sustained a high demand, bearings then required for military equipment.

By the late Forties Tony Vandervell's Park Royal, Acton (West London) based company was a huge concern. Since the BRM project was slow moving, in 1949 Vandervell purchased a 1.5 litre Ferrari Grand Prix car as a means of further assisting the effort, and for the sport of it. Unlike Lucas and Owen, Vandervell was a motor racing enthusiast through and through. Purchase of the car was not a straightforward business, though. It required an import licence, while the export of currency also required special permission. Vandervell argued that the car would form an ideal test bed for his bearings, and the fact that his company supplied the Ministry of Defence can have done his case no harm at all.

The 1.5 litre supercharged Ferrari was the first Grand Prix car to be fitted with Thinwall bearings. Vandervell was permitted to pay Ferrari the princely sum of £5430 in return for an example, which came with a handful of spares and tools, including a couple of wheels and a couple of pistons. Vandervell dubbed his Ferrari the 'Thinwall Special' and entered it for the British Grand Prix at Silverstone, where both Mays and BRM Head Mechanic Richardson drove it. Partly due to a very short wheelbase, it proved tricky to handle and Richardson - who had no racing experience - crashed it out of the race.

Vandervell subsequently sent the car back to Italy with a detailed engineering report by Berthon and a covering note in which he described his disappointment at the performance of his expensive acquisition. Since Vandervell supplied Ferrari with bearings the Italian team was keen to stay in favour with him. Following long discussions over the winter of '49/'50 Vandervell agreed to take delivery of an improved, longer wheelbase machine for 1950 and this appeared at Silverstone in Ferrari driver Alberto Ascari's hands.

Again the so called Thinwall Special proved a disappointment, Ascari spun off in a cloudburst and again the car went back to the factory after only one outing, its purchaser disgruntled. Vandervell's Research and Development Department had stripped the Ferrari and Vandervell did not like the standard of engineering to be found within the engine. That much he made clear to Enzo Ferrari, who was not accustomed to such knowledgeable feedback from customers.

Meanwhile, the BRM had made its first racing appearance, likewise in the Silverstone race. In the words of Mays: "When the flag fell, Sommer let in the clutch. There was a dull metallic crunch. The BRM jerked forward two inches and stopped dead".

Towards the end of the season the BRM came out again, at Goodwood. This time it won. Indeed, it won both short races on offer that memorable day, but they were very minor affairs. The real test against some of Italy's finest came at Barcelona in late October. Two V16 cars ran, proving fast but fragile. The season ended without the widely anticipated glorious defeat of the red machines. This came as no surprise to realistic racing insiders but in the eyes of countless outsiders the nationally supported project had again been a let down.

Media criticism was widespread, largely unfair and a good proportion of it was cruel. Hype had turned to ridicule. The key movers retained faith, however. The Trust was re-organised over the winter with a slimmer, five man steering committee consisting of Owen, Lucas' representative Bernard Scott, Vandervell, Mays and Berthon. The same quintet now formed the Board of the BRM company.

Although the British motor industry re-doubled its financial support, for various reasons preparations for the 1951 season were delayed. Indeed, sluggish progress had become characteristic of the entire project, the engineering of which was far sighted but very ambitious. Due to engine development headaches the team did not emerge before the British Grand Prix in July and then the extremely complex cars had to be run on reduced boost.

In the meantime Vandervell's Ferrari had been rebuilt at Maranello as a 4.5 litre unsupercharged V12 machine with a further modified chassis. This followed factory development for 1951. The green painted car - still known as the Thinwall Special - had won a rain-disrupted International Trophy race at Silverstone in May. At Silverstone for the British Grand Prix the car was in mid grid, Gonzalez' unblown works Ferrari was on pole, BRM missed practice. On race day Gonzalez took a historic victory over the 1.5 litre supercharged Alfa Romeos while BRM still floundered. The era of supercharging was drawing to a close. At the Nurburgring and at Monza Ascari's factory 4.5 litre Ferrari won...

At Monza the difficult BRM V16 re-appeared, only to have to withdraw due to a gearbox defect. Further '51 outings were scrapped. Over the winter Vandervell resigned from the project. Mays later wrote: "Unfortunately Vandervell and I could not get on together; we both seemed to rub each other the wrong way".

Vandervell could see the way the wind of technical change was blowing and he had his own ideas for beating the red cars. These were based on an entirely different game plan, though the goal of putting British Racing Green to the fore remained the same. Vandervell was a patriot through and through.

Vandervell's departure emphasised the inherent drawback of any committee managed racing project. In a nutshell, it lacks responsiveness (and often it lacks direction). Meanwhile, Owen remarked: "My confidence in the BRM remains absolutely unshaken. It is, I believe, a basically sound engineering concept, a clear two years ahead of any known rival in its design. It is admittedly unfortunate that its growing pains should have been so prolonged, and criticism on that score is certainly admissible".

There was another snag. It had now been announced that a new formula would take effect from January 1954, this catering for 2.5 litres unsupercharged or 750cc. supercharged cars. The advanced V16 engine had only two years active life left. Worse, with the withdrawal of the Alfa Romeo team the British car was the only serious challenger to Ferrari for 1952. Before the season got underway came news from France that the oldest Grand Prix of all would be held to Formula Two regulations. Understandably, the continentals did not rate the BRM as a serious obstacle to a Ferrari whitewash. Other organisers followed suit. Thus the 1952 World Championship became a Formula Two - 2.0 litre unsupercharged - contest.

That suited Vandervell's strategy. Central to his approach was a switch to a simple unblown car. Where BRM had championed a complex V16 supercharged design - powerful but fraught with development difficulties - Vandervell looked to a practical four cylinder engine. On the face of it, moving to normal aspiration made a multiplicity of cylinders essential. More cylinders means less stress for a given speed, hence a higher speed potential. Without forced induction, surely engine speed was even more important - after all, is not power a function of b.m.e.p. and speed?

It is, but it is important to remember that b.m.e.p. tends to fall as speed rises. At this stage in the development of the normally aspirated racing engine, breathing started to become a problem at speeds in excess of 7,000r.p.m. The 4.5 litre unblown V12 Ferrari that had overthrown the establishment ran to only 7,500r.p.m. Remember that supercharging had been in vogue for around three decades so the art of breathing without assistance had for a long time been somewhat neglected.

Further, the disadvantage of an engine built primarily to chase speed tended to be a narrow power band. The main problem for a normally aspirated engine is that as speed rises there is a shorter time interval between succeeding impulses in which aspiration can take place, hence volumetric (breathing) efficiency tends to fall off. Further, increasing speed demands bigger ports and valves and these may not be able to accelerate the airflow at lower engine speeds well enough to produce the turbulence necessary for good combustion.

Also to be considered are the mechanical difficulties associated with high speed. The 1.5 litre BRM had tiny 93.75cc. cylinders - a V16 of 2.5 litre displacement would have 156.25cc. cylinders and consequently far greater crankcase, crankshaft, con rod and bearing stress for a given engine speed. Further, the greater inertia of its necessarily larger valves would make it far more prone to valve train stress failure. Then there was the problem of ensuring a strong and reliable spark, contemporary magneto systems hard pressed to cope with high four figure, let alone five figure engine speeds.

Running to a five figure speed and blown to 5.0 bar absolute the BRM engine had managed to produce over 500b.h.p. at the expense of high mechanical and thermal stress and of an extremely narrow power band. BRM had 500 wild, untamed horses. Running less revs and less boost the more manageable rival Italian supercharged engines had produced around 400b.h.p. from 1.5 litres and the unblown 4.5 litre Ferrari came close to matching that figure. At this stage the 80b.h.p. per litre of the '51 Ferrari V12 was typical of a normally aspirated car racing engine but 100b.h.p. per litre was known in the motorcycle world where supercharging had not dominated inter-war development.

Logically, given a three times displacement equivalence formula the normally aspirated route had greater potential than the established supercharged route. From 1954 the equivalence ratio would be further in favour of the 'atmos' at three and a third times. Aware of this, Vandervell reasoned that a simple, well designed four cylinder engine running to 7,500r.p.m. could provide adequate power with more useable power than a supercharged engine.

Its simplicity would allow its engineers to get on with development engineering rather than troubleshooting. Not only that, but Vandervell was astute enough to realise that much of that development work would centre on the contribution of the fuel chemist. Given normal aspiration and the mechanical difficulties posed by high speed running, it was obvious that the vital performance factor - more important even than engine speed (due to the breathing difficulties posed by high revolutions) - would be the brew it was fed.

There was nothing new in fuel trickery - methanol was the staple diet of the supercharged engine, which with increasing boost had become dependent upon alcohol's high resistance to detonation and its internal cooling properties. Methanol - methyl (wood) alcohol - has a far lower calorific value than petrol so a good deal more needs to be burned. However, the fact that it is run richer together with its high latent heat of evaporation and its high resistance to detonation allow far higher compression ratios to be run, yielding greater power.

In 1951 the Grand Prix world was only just starting to re-discover the potential of a methanol fuelled normally aspirated engine. However, as we have noted, the motorcycle racing world had continued to progress unblown racing engine development. Vandervell was a director of Norton, his father the Chairman. Indeed, Guy Anthony had grown up riding Norton motorcycles. In the Thirties and Forties racing 500cc. motorcycles led the unsupercharged automotive field in terms of power per litre and Norton had long been the most successful manufacturer. Vandervell had the idea of basing a four cylinder power plant on the single cylinder Norton engine.

Earlier, Vandervell had suggested that BRM design a four cylinder, 500cc. spin off of its V16 engine for Norton to try as a motorcycle racing engine. This project got nowhere as BRM struggled to sort its complex Formula One car. That was no great loss since the Norton single continued to rule the roost into the Fifties under the guidance of Chief Engineer Joe Craig and Development Engineer Leo Kuzmicki. Talking to Craig and Kuzmicki had led Vandervell to the idea of a 2.0 litre four cylinder car version of the Norton single.

Back in the Forties, as part of the Norton-BRM project BRM had done tests comparing the standard air cooled Norton single with a water cooled version, both running the low octane 'pool' petrol of the day. At 7,000r.p.m. the air cooled version produced 44.2 b.h.p, the water cooled version 47 b.h.p. thanks to a higher compression ratio. That figure from half a litre on very poor petrol was food for thought, contemporary Formula Two engines hard pressed to reach 47b.h.p. per half litre on exotic fuel.

Conveniently, the swing to Formula Two meant that Vandervell could start off with effectively four Norton 'wet' engines in line on a common bottom end for the mandatory 2.0 litre maximum. The contemporary Ferrari Formula Two car gave around 180b.h.p. Vandervell could hope to see in excess of 200b.h.p. and with fuel technology playing a key role he felt that he had enough cylinders for long term development. At this stage Ferrari was moving from twelve to four cylinders, in search of better breathing. The V12 required six carburettors and complex inlet plumbing that spoiled volumetric efficiency.

Late in '51 Vandervell set up his own engine design group at Park Royal, working closely with the family's Norton factory. Park Royal had an extensive design and drawing office and one of the finest tool rooms in Britain. Engineering Manager Freddie Fox was appointed general overseer of the racing car project, the cost of which was absorbed by Vandervell Products' R&D budget. To help keep the project secret, many acquisition orders were placed through Norton. Former BRM Chief Designer Eric Richter joined the engine design team.

Of course, there was a tremendous amount of work involved in the move from Norton single motorcycle to four cylinder car engine so development of Vandervell's Norton derivative would take time, as would production of a suitable chassis. In the meantime Vandervell continued the Thinwall Special programme, taking delivery of yet another 4.5 litre Ferrari. To run this, a racing car preparation 'shop was set up at Park Royal. Running the car allowed Vandervell to try out its own chassis ideas. The Italian car was campaigned mainly in British Formula Libre events in '52.

Shut out of World Championship races, BRM had to look to such meetings to keep the V16s running. Its season started at Albi in France, then moved to Dundrod in Ireland, thence to Silverstone where a Formula Libre race supported the Formula Two regulation Grand Prix event. At Silverstone BRM suffered its third successive defeat of the season: on this occasion Piero Taruffi won in the Thinwall Special. BRM failed again at Boreham, then won at Turnberry following a gearbox problem for the Vandervell car, which this weekend was driven by Mike Hawthorn.

Success had come too late for the BRM project: short of funds and unable to contest World Championship Grands Prix, the Trust was wound up and the BRM company was sold off. Vandervell expressed an interest in acquiring the assets of BRM, should there be no other offers. There were other offers and the best came from Owen. So it was that two of Britain's most powerful industrialists lined up against each other in 1953 Formula Libre events.

This year the green painted Ferrari was fitted with new-fangled disc brakes, as pioneered by the BRM V16 in '52. Vandervell had seen the potential of both disc brakes and fuel injection, technology developed by the aircraft industry. Disc brakes offered relatively fade free operation compared to the normal hydraulically operated drum systems thanks to the inherently superior heat dissipation of the exposed disc, with less heat transferred to the tyre and an unsprung weight saving. Fuel injection offers the potential for unrestricted porting and for improved fuelling, for a sophisticated system can match fuel delivery to both engine speed and load. Carburettors that provided an adequate choke size for high speed operation tended towards the formation of fuel droplets in the inlet tract at low to medium speed operation.

Back in '51 Vandervell had enquired disc brakes of the aircraft industry. Goodyear had been keen to help, whereas BRM had looked to Girling. Goodyear designed disc brakes were made at Park Royal. The discs were steel forgings rather than cast iron and were drilled radially to help dissipate heat and save weight. The calipers were pivoted on one side and only one pad moved, this squeezing the disc onto the pad the other side.

Meanwhile, for the new Vandervell engine fuel injection was under investigation. Park Royal looked at the new constant flow Hilborn system used in Indy Car racing but it was considered too crude, and at the Bosch system introduced with the '53 Mercedes 300SL sports car. Bosch offered a sophisticated pump providing timed squirts of fuel at high pressure into the manifold or directly into the cylinder, the straight line delivery characteristics of the engine driven pump overridden according to inputs from a load sensor. This system was considered promising and discussions commenced with Bosch.

At the outset in '53 the Thinwall Special was driven by Guiseppe Farina. Round one at Goodwood fell to BRM. The next clash was at Albi, for which event the Vandervell team made a rare trip abroad while Ferrari wheeled out a dusted-off 4.5 litre factory car. Both it and the Thinwall Special broke: at last BRM took a win over the Italians. In the heat. In the final, without serious opposition, BRM again failed to deliver, this time due to tyre trouble.

Silverstone was next: Vandervell versus Owen went to the former. Then Charterhall went to the latter, Goodwood to the former. This time Hawthorn was Park Royal's victor, the young English Ferrari works driver back with the team, replacing the veteran Farina. So it was that, as in 1952, the Thinwall Special took two victories. The main development headache had been the gearbox which lacked the strength necessary to cope with the torque of the 4.5 litre engine. The 'box thus became a Vandervell development of the Ferrari original while Ferrari produced its own strengthened transaxle for its rarely seen works Formula One cars.

Meanwhile, during its two interim years of Formula Two regulations the World Championship had been dominated by the Ferrari. British representatives had been numerous, including Alta, Alta-HWM, Bristol-Cooper and Connaught to name but four of a crop of underpowered cars. It had taken the resurgence of Maserati in '53 to loosen the Maranello grip. Vandervell had yet to air his 2.0 litre project. Ever pragmatic, he was not going to show his hand until he was ready. He had seen the BRM run before it was ready...

Both BRM and Vandervell were now planning 2.5 litre designs. With the advent of the 2.5 litre Formula One, Grand Prix racing was getting serious again. Ferrari and Maserati were ready to continue battle with 2.5 litre unsupercharged cars while Lancia and Daimler-Benz were finalising new designs, similarly taking the unblown route. This was the first time since the war that a good number of marques had produced brand new Grand Prix engines.

Since it was established by the motorcycle world that an unblown engine could produce 100 b.h.p. per litre given unrestricted fuel, the target was 250b.h.p. In the Forties the 500cc. Norton single had produced 50b.h.p. on methanol, more on stronger brews including nitromethane which has a damaging effect on engine internals. Clearly, for mid Fifties Grand Prix participation a serious commitment to engine development was required and the participation of four major marques left little room for the small fry.

The various British Formula Two constructors were unable to contemplate serious participation. Connaught planned to struggle on regardless, upgrading its existing equipment in the face of inadequate finance. Sadly, a 2.5 litre version of the old production-based Alta four did not promise much in excess of 200b.h.p. Britain's real hope lay in the resources of Owen and Vandervell. Both planned carefully to develop their brand new designs, both of which were for four cylinder cars targeted at an initial 250b.h.p.

The Vandervell family had now sold its interest in Norton but Craig and Kuzmicki and others in the firm's racing department continued to lend assistance to the Park Royal engine project. At the same time Cooper designer Owen Maddock was drawing a suitable chassis, Vandervell having commissioned John Cooper to provide a frame. The first 2.0 litre engine was bench tested late in '53 and work had already started on a 2.5 litre derivative.

At Bourne, BRM philosophy now echoed that of Vandervell. Mays remarked: "we had learned the hard way that it is the speed at which you can develop and improve that counts - hence the choice of a simple four cylinder unblown engine". The BRM did not emerge in 1954, though the V16 car continued to battle the Thinwall Special in British Formula Libre events. Peter Collins drove the 4.5 litre Vandervell Ferrari and gave it three more wins in '54 home races. Meantime, the so called Vanwall Special came out in 2.0 litre guise for the Silverstone International Trophy Formula One race on May 15.

Back in February Vandervell had written to Kuzmicki to report: "we have done it... we have 235b.h.p. at 7,500-7,600r.p.m. without a potent fuel mix and with 29" straight exhaust pipes and we ran to 7,800r.p.m. without damage". A figure of 235b.h.p. is hard to believe considering that the contemporary Maserati 250F gave no more than that from 2.5 litres. The Park Royal engine was as strong as the Norton might have been on methanol and with water cooling and reflected the latest Norton racing practice with cylinder dimensions of 85.9mm. x 86mm. It had Norton's design of porting and hemispherical combustion chamber with two valves for each cylinder and the same 77 degrees included valve angle.

Unlike the motorcycle engine, it had twin plugs fired by a pair of Scintilla magnetos. Following Norton practice, the valves were operated by twin overhead camshafts (these gear driven off the front of the crankshaft) and were closed by hairpin springs. Exposed, these springs and unusual Amal carburettors (one per cylinder as a stopgap until fuel injection was ready) told of the motorcycle heritage. While the upper part of the engine was Norton-inspired, the bottom end was based on a Rolls Royce crankcase and whereas Norton ran roller bearings at the big end, Vandervell employed its own Thinwall shell bearings, hence a split con rod but a one-piece crankshaft.

First appeara
the Vanwall
as a 2.3 litre ca
at the 1954
Grand Prix,
Collins was
end runner.
the new d
over the surfa
diator
clearly spoile
airflow over th
of the car,
causing a grea
of drag. Howev
must have crea
measu
downforce

The castings and forgings came from a variety of suppliers, some associated with Norton, all working to Vandervell drawings. Both the Norton head design and the Rolls Royce crankcase pattern had to be adapted to suit the new requirements. Vandervell ensured there was enough 'meat' in its castings to go to 96 x 86mm. for 2.5 litres in due course and Cooper had been asked to provide for a 2.5 litre engine output. Cooper supplied the bare frame, Walter Potter did additional fabrication work, George Gray fabricated the bodywork and the car was built up in the Vandervell tool room.

The new Vanwall chassis was clearly derived from the stable's green Ferraris. It featured a conventional tubular ladder frame, wishbone front suspension, de Dion rear with leaf springs both ends and a four speed gearbox mounted in unit with the differential. All this was Ferrari practice and Maddock had been asked to incorporate Ferrari suspension, steering and transmission parts. The single seater body was conventional and the most unusual aspects of the chassis were Goodyear-designed disc brakes, as already seen on the Thinwall Special, and an arrangement of external gilled tubes which acted as the radiator.

The disc brakes had proved powerful, reliable and fade free on the Thinwall Special. Nevertheless, continental Formula One cars universally continued to rely upon drums. The gilled tube system avoided the discharge of hot air into the engine bay, ensuring a supply of cool air for the carburettors. With a four into one exhaust system the new car proved surprisingly quiet. It had first run at RAF Odiham near Basingstoke, then further tests had been carried out at Goodwood.

Driven by Formula Two exponent Alan Brown, at Silverstone the very driveable new Vandervell creation was fastest in the second day's damp practice. In spite of aquaplaning into a spin

at Monza
Vanwall Spe-
: its first
s expedition.
ngine was still
litre interim
t this time it
fail, Collins
g seventh.
he reversion to
entional front
r in the
of enhanced
.

Brown finished sixth in his heat - the first 2.0 litre car home - but the car retired from the final with a broken oil pipe when lying fifth. Fitted with a new 91mm. bore 2.3 litre interim engine and aluminium ducting over the surface radiator, the Pirelli shod machine re-appeared for the British Grand Prix at Silverstone driven by Collins. Collins qualified 17th for the World Championship event, four seconds off Moss' Maserati pole time. Cylinder head water joint leakage sidelined the car after 17 laps. Wills pressure rings sealed the head and in the light of the problem Wills set to work on an improved seal.

Undaunted, Vandervell sent the car off to Monza for the Italian Grand Prix in early September. This time Collins was 16th on the grid, six seconds off Fangio's pole time but he finished, in seventh place five laps down after an oil feed to the pressure gauge cracked, releasing vital lubricant. The car now had a conventional radiator but was still running the interim engine, the 2.5 litre version having broken a valve on test. Since this version - only the third engin constructed - sported a 96mm. bore it had a modified combustion chamber shape. This entailed a revision of the valve angle, which was reduced to 60 degrees included.

By the time the larger unit was ready to race it was September. Keen to get racing mileage on it, Vandervell ran the one-off Vanwall Special in lesser events at Goodwood and Aintree. Although it did not win any of the races on offer at these second string events, Peter Collins bagged a second place at Goodwood, Hawthorn at Aintree and the overall impression was distinctly favourable, certainly in the eyes of success-starved English observers.

It was now late October and there was one Grand Prix still to run, the Spanish event at Barcelona. Vandervell shipped the car out, again

for Collins. Alas, he crashed out in practice. Forced to spectate, he saw the new Lancia show a flash of promise, the Mercedes team strangely off form: the season ended with a Ferrari victory for his great friend Hawthorn. But the new World Champion drove for Daimler-Benz. With Ferrari, Maserati and Lancia also strong it was clear that 1955 was shaping up as a battle of four continental marques: Italy versus Germany.

Undaunted by the high power opposition and a lack of experience of three hour races, Vandervell planned an extensive Grand Prix campaign for 1955. He abandoned the Thinwall Special Ferrari and signed Hawthorn, luring him from Ferrari. The team was to run two Vanwalls (the Special tag was dropped) with Ken Wharton the second driver following an abortive attempt to retain Collins. The ambitious team set out to contest all the European based Grands Prix, following a warm up outing in the International Trophy.

The car crashed in Spain was not rebuilt and Vandervell produced four new chassis, again with conventional radiators, the tubular affair having been blamed for some of the early engine troubles. In late '54 he had been supplied with a regular customer 250F, which was studied closely but was not raced. Meanwhile, following the closure of the Norton racing department by its new owners, Kuzmicki had joined Vandervell as a research engineer.

The '55 power plant was an injected version of the 2.5 litre engine. Bosch direct injection had been used by Daimler-Benz in Formula One 1954. Exploiting his connections in the German motor industry which he supplied with bearings, Vandervell had received his first bespoke four cylinder Bosch injection pump in '54. The British engine was equipped with an indirect injection system, the injectors feeding into the inlet tracts across the flow close to the valve, the valve assisting atomisation.

A four cylinder engine was a new experience for Bosch, and a headache at that due to its significantly greater vibration which played havoc with the high pressure feed lines. Further, it was found that the induction pressure sensors used to measure load led to poor throttle response. Vandervell substituted a direct mechanical linkage between the throttles and the pump, the pump mounted on the front of the engine, driven from the timing gears.

For '55 more potent fuel was introduced, again a mixture of methanol and Avgas, the former ranging from one to two thirds of the whole. Methanol reduced internal temperatures but increased fuel consumption. Too much heat caused the heads of the sodium cooled exhaust valves to fall off. Valve and head temperatures were crucial and another development headache was broken valve springs due to the inertia of the large, thus heavy valves. Meanwhile the chassis engineers made modifications, the handling and roadholding having been found wanting in '54. Most obvious were coil springs at the front and an inboard location for the rear brakes.

Both injected Vanwalls retired from the Silverstone season opener, Hawthorn with a gearbox oil leak, Wharton crashing following a stuck throttle, the accident leaving him with burns. Thus, Hawthorn alone started the Monaco Grand Prix, only to retire, a ball joint in the throttle/pump linkage shattering. At Spa Francorchamps he again retired after a multitude of practice problems, including a clutch cooked when G.A.V. drove the car from Spa to the circuit. Having been off the pace, Hawthorn rejoined Ferrari, while Vandervell missed the Dutch Grand Prix for much needed development time.

For the British Grand Prix at Aintree Vandervell fielded Wharton and Harry Schell, neither a driver of Hawthorn's calibre. Schell's car stalled at the start, he got going dead last and tore through the back markers, going on to pass the entire Ferrari team before the throttle pedal broke. The Franco-American then took over Wharton's machine which had pitted with a broken oil line, impressing by running in company with the leading Mercedes for several laps. He brought the car home ninth, 18 laps down, his pace a big boost for team morale.

Too many teething troubles were bugging the Vanwall project, though the car had started to show promise in Schell's enthusiastic hands. The engine power was clearly adequate but the roadholding still left something to be desired.

With the cancellation of the French and German Grands Prix in the wake of the '55 Le Mans disaster, only Monza was left on the Grand Prix calendar and Vandervell again looked to a number

e 1955 International Trophy at Silstone: Ken arton before and r his nasty nt in the second litre Vanwall cial. The fire ead throughout car, which was s written off, harton escaping h some nasty ns that kept him of racing for a ile.

of lesser British races to gain competitive track time. Schell finished second at Crystal Palace, then won at Snetterton with Wharton second. These successes were further boosts for morale but against negligible opposition counted for little.

At Monza there was a third, spare car while a faired windscreen and front suspension cowls helped reduce drag but the latter had to be removed since bigger front wheels proved necessary on the banking. The plucky Schell again impressed but he was nine seconds from Fangio's pole time and both cars went out early on. The season finished with a trio of minor races back in England, two of which - on the same day at Castle Coombe - were won by Schell. The Vanwall was a good second string Formula One car but it was not yet a serious Grand Prix force. Neither was the Connaught, while the new four cylinder BRM had raced in only one event towards the end of the season. Impressive on that occasion, it was an unproven quantity.

At the end of the season Daimler-Benz quit motor racing, as Lancia had done mid way through the year. That left Ferrari and Maserati as the establishment, the three British marques and Gordini the applicants to its ranks. Daimler-Benz' departure left Moss free and all the British teams requested his services. Moss tried the three cars and found the Connaught heavy and under-powered, the quicker Vanwall heavy but easier to handle than the BRM, with which he could make a comparable lap time. None of the trio were obvious world beaters. Following a poll of 17 motoring journalists, Moss took the majority verdict and signed for Maserati.

Keen to improve his chances for 1956, Vandervell drafted in young engineers Frank Costin and Colin Chapman to attend, respectively, to aerodynamics and chassis design. An aircraft man, Costin had designed aerodynamic bodies for Chapman's Lotus concern and had been responsible for the Monza fairings. After Monza, he had met Vandervell again at a garage in Chester where the cars were stripped down undergoing preparation for running at nearby Oulton Park. Vandervell asked him his opinion

of them. Costin pointed to the engine and said, "that's great - but the rest is a heap of ****"...

"Can you do any better", asked Vandervell. "Yes". "Well you'd better do something about it then".

Costin reflected on the challenge and reasoned that his friend Chapman should do the frame and suspension since he had more practical experience of racing car load inputs. Costin's experience was largely of aeroplanes and Vandervell appreciated that he could offer a state of the art aircraft approach to the challenge of drag reduction. But Costin would not commit until Chapman was confirmed for the mechanicals. Soon the message came through from Vandervell's office: "I've got him - you can start".

Meanwhile, the withdrawal of Daimler-Benz had released a number of Bosch fuel injection specialists to help hone the engine. The Vanwall four was powerful and it was Vandervell's view that with further refinement and an improved chassis his car could be the basis of a Grand Prix winner. Few could argue with that assessment of the project. Vandervell duly expanded his operation to a three car capability, looking to match the efforts of the Italian teams. Lacking only an established Ace, this was the sort of serious challenge to the Reds that the original BRM project had professed to make ten years earlier.

Fuel injection (pictured here on a 2.5 litre engine) and disc brakes (previous spread) were major innovations in the mid Fifties. Vandervell was keen to exploit both developments. Note the fairing behind the disc: this was a Costin innovation for Monza, but it had to be discarded due to a switch to 17" wheels. Also on the previous spread, Schell is pictured on the Monza banking.

56

In The Stable

If the 1956 Vanwall bid had an obvious weakness, it was in its lack of a top line driver. World Champion Fangio - Vandervell's first choice - had signed for Ferrari while, as we have seen, Moss had opted for Maserati. Of the other British drivers, the leading lights were Hawthorn and Collins while the name on everyone's lips was that of Tony Brooks, the newcomer having given Connaught a sensational end of season victory in a non-Championship race at Syracuse. BRM signed both Hawthorn and Brooks while Collins took over where Hawthorn had left off at Ferrari.

Vandervell retained the plucky Schell and signed Ferrari regular Maurice Trintignant to partner him. Trintignant had never been the quickest of Maranello's mid Fifties squad but he was a highly experienced Grand Prix driver who could be relied upon to do a solid job. After the disappointments of '55 Vandervell was not expecting to mount a serious challenge for the World Championship title, rather to amass the experience that he would need to support a top line driver the following season.

Four new chassis were built to the design of Costin and Chapman, plated VW1/56 to VW4/56. Costin had no formal contract with the Vandervell only word of mouth and was working in his spare time, by day running de Havilland's flight test department. Chapman's relationship was more formal, chassis building his bread and butter. Chapman was racing enthusiast through and through, and no mean driver at that. Costin was an aircraft man who believed that racing could and would improve road car design. He was also attracted by the fact that it provided more scope than the world of aviation for individual flair and creativity.

The revamped Vanwall faced a known quantity in the '56 machines from Ferrari and Maserati, the latter similarly Pirelli shod. Pirelli tyres were generally considered superior to the Engelberts run by Ferrari and the Dunlops common in England, Vandervell again exploiting his European motor industry connections. Ferrari was retaining a modified version of the Lancia V8 it had been handed the previous year while Maserati was continuing to develop its familiar 250F in line six. BRM was a dark horse while Gordini was the only other marque committed to a World Championship campaign and its ageing six cylinder machine was somewhat outclassed. Sadly, Connaught's plans were similarly thwarted by financial difficulties.

Vandervell planned to concentrate solely upon World Championship events in 1956, though he did not intend to contest the Argentine Grand Prix, the new car unready. Chapman and Costin worked fast but Costin had not received Chapman's rapidly conceived general arrangement drawing much before Christmas 1955. Instead, three striking, radically streamlined machines were readied for the start of the European season in May.

The racing preparation department at Park Royal was known as "The Stable" and employed over a dozen mechanics under Frank Davis. Fox was still Engineering Manager - working with the R&D department - while the Team Manager was David Yorke. Chassis consultant Chapman was slated as a possible third Vanwall driver, though the team was to concentrate upon Schell and Trintignant.

One week before the first European Grand Prix at Monte Carlo was the International Trophy at Silverstone and since this was the circuit due to host the British Grand Prix Vandervell made the race an exception to his Grand Prix only rule. Not only would the International Trophy provide valuable practice, it would also give Vanwall the chance to work with Moss, since Maserati did not intend to field a works car. Further feedback from Moss could only strengthen the team and it could also help lead to an association in the longer term. Vandervell and Moss shared a common desire to put the green to the fore.

Guy Anthony Vandervell as enthusiasts will remember him - in the prime of his life, proudly overseeing the Vanwall team in the Grand Prix paddock.

Over a Barrel

96.0 x 86mm./ 2490cc.
Unblown
Aluminium alloy crankcase and head
Wet cast iron liners
5 main bearings, plain
Steel crankshaft, 4 pins
Steel con rods
Hepworth light alloy pistons
Hepworth rings
D.o.h.c., gear driven
2 valves/cylinder, 2 plugs
60 degree included valve angle
1.90in. inlet valve, 1.70in. exhaust
Bosch ignition
Bosch injection
Compression ratio 12.5:1
164kg.

In moving to 96mm. x 86mm. for 2490cc, the Vanwall's stroke to bore ratio had fallen to 0.9:1, whereas it had started life as a Norton-dimensioned square engine. The move to over-square dimensions, while fashionable and in the interest of plenty of valve area had made provision of a satisfactory combustion chamber shape more difficult given a high compression ratio. In simple terms, as the head's hemisphere grew in size, so did the dome on the piston, to the detriment of surface to volume ratio.

Nevertheless, around the non-Norton 60 degree included valve angle Vandervell's engineers had managed to produce a good twin plug chamber, as was evident from the competitive output of the '55 engine. The two valves were each inclined at 30 degrees from the vertical with an offset from the central axis of the cylinder of approximately 0.01in. to the exhaust side, this to accommodate a larger inlet valve. With a compression ratio exceeding 12.0:1 the piston had a pronounced dome in which there were deep valve clearance cut outs.

Good breathing and good burning are vital performance factors and combustion chamber and porting design are of paramount importance. Of course, the Vanwall four was based on well proven porting, the Norton single noted for its breathing ability. Further, the Norton had been carefully developed to take full advantage from inlet tuning on pressure wave principles.

Pressure waves travel up and down the inlet tract and it is possible to harness the energy present in those waves to aid induction. The object is to dimension the inlet pipes so that they resonate at the region of engine speed at which improved induction is most wanted. The effect of the resonance is to induce better filling of the cylinder since higher than atmospheric pressure is generated above the valve. This technique had

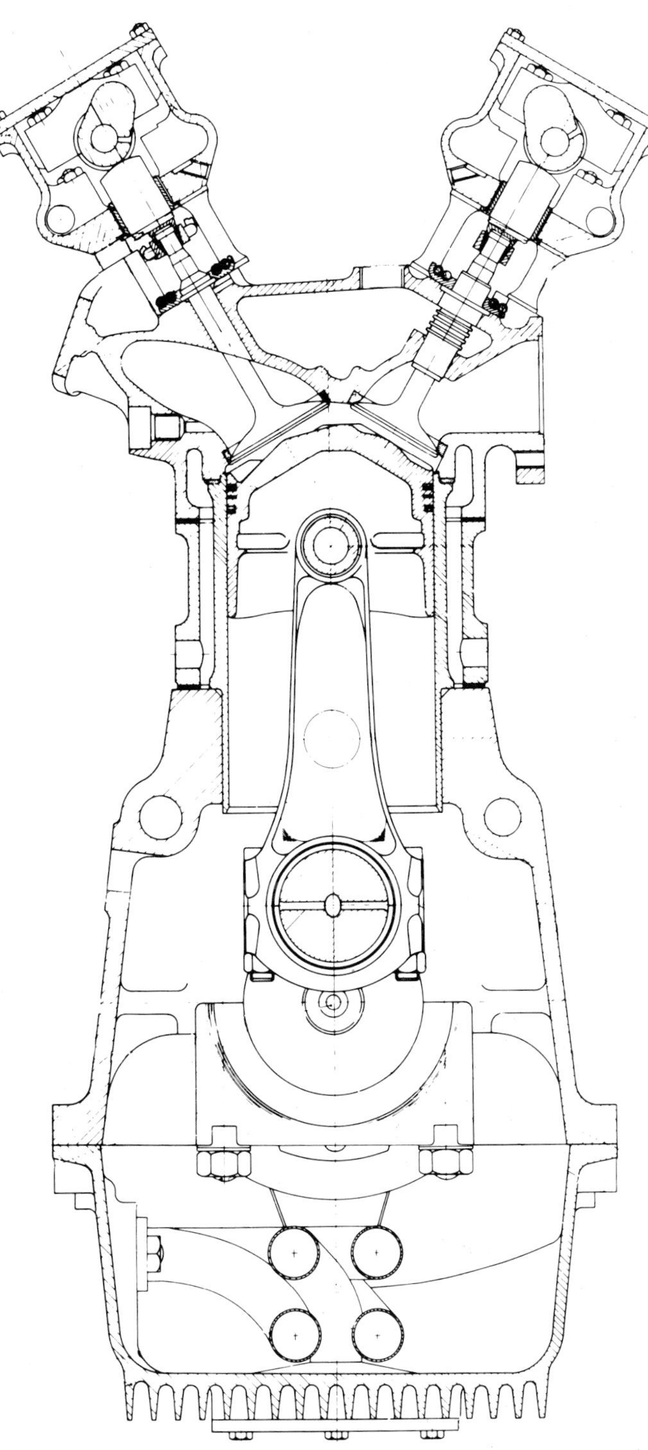

already been tried by Connaught and HWM on respectively Lea Francis and Alta Formula Two engines and was longer established in motorcycle racing, Norton in the vanguard.

The '56 version of the injected Vanwall engine was immediately distinguishable by flared trumpets fitted to the Amal carburettor bodies that had been retained to provide the throttles. These new trumpets were part of the on going process of inlet tuning. Popular in motorcycle racing, the Amal design of carburettor body offered an unobstructed bore at full throttle, hence its retention.

Although having only four cylinders, as we have noted the new Vanwall engine was designed to run to a speed in excess of 7,000r.p.m. Nevertheless, with its relatively large, heavy pistons a four cylinder engine clearly could not hope to match the speed attainable by an equivalent displacement six or eight cylinder engine. Maserati had six cylinders, Daimler-Benz and Lancia eight. However, as we have noted higher speed is not an automatic gain and in the mid Fifties it was not of paramount concern. The exploitation of increasingly potent fuel was.

Consider that the Maserati straight six had started life in '54 producing 220b.h.p. running to 7,400r.p.m. on a compression ratio of 11.0:1 and 50% methanol, blended with petrol. By '56 the engine was not running significantly faster - only just exceeding 8,000 r.p.m. - but it was pumping out in excess of 270b.h.p. thanks largely to improved fuel. In terms of power per litre per 1000r.p.m. it had jumped from 11.9b.h.p. to 13.5b.h.p. as the brew strengthened and the compression ratio increased.

The '56 Vanwall engine ran on a mixture of methanol and petrol/benzole and a compression ratio in the region of 12.0 - 13.0:1. Following winter development work power was quoted as 280b.h.p. at 7,400r.p.m. with b.m.e.p. in the region of 220 - 225 lb./sq.in. all the way through from 4,000 r.p.m. to the peak power engine speed. That performance was a significant increase over '55. The peak power reading represented an output of 112b.h.p. per litre and 15.14b.h.p. per litre per 1000r.p.m. - a most impressive figure.

The strong Vanwall engine was constructed with detachable crankcase and head, as the Norton original. Indeed, it was constructed as four independent cylinders within a common water jacket and topped by a common head. Wet iron cylinder liners (from Wellworthy of Lymington) were spigoted firmly into a barrel-type crankcase. The top of the crankcase was over 60mm. thick and the liners were spigoted for over one third of their length. The surrounding head and water jacket castings were aluminium alloy - RR50 - as was the sturdy crankcase - RR53B - from which ten high tensile tie rods ran to the head.

Indeed, the tie rods ran right from the main bearing caps to the tappet blocks. They clamped the entire engine structure together. The liners were sandwiched between crankcase and head, with ring sealing for each liner/head joint. To ensure a good seal Cooper Mechanical Joints had devised a stainless steel ring joint with internal corrugations. There were rubber water sealing joints for the water jacket's crankcase and head interfaces, the jacket not a fully stressed member of the engine structure.

A four cylinder in line engine with a 'mirror image' flat plane crankshaft is balanced for primary forces but suffers a secondary imbalance, pronounced where the stroke:bore ratio is high, as in this case. The vibration of the Vanwall unit particularly affected ancillaries (for example, the vibration was a headache for Bosch, as we have noted). Within the engine the imbalance manifested itself as a side to side shake of the crankshaft. This caused high internal stresses which needed to be contained by the crankcase.

Vandervell had found a suitably robust crankcase in the Rolls Royce B40 four bearing iron monobloc, the barrel crankcase of which extended well below the crankshaft centreline. Leyland Motors provided the patterns and cores and the Vandervell drawing office made the necessary modifications for it to be cast in aluminium without its block by the Aeroplane and Motor Ltd. company of Coventry (which did all the major castings for the engine).

The crankcase was closed by a deep light alloy sump. For the 2.3 litre and subsequent 2.5 litre engines Vandervell added a fifth main bearing rather than have flying middle throws. In contrast, the BRM four cylinder engine ran only three main bearings.

At the top end of the Vanwall engine the legacy of the Norton engine was still evident in the unfashionable exposed hairpin valve springs. Mind you, the deployment of hairpin valve springs followed Ferrari as well as motorcycle racing practice. In theory the hairpin type spring offered lower inertial weight than a coil, this factor promising better reliability at high r.p.m. However, it was difficult to ensure a good surface finish and since the spring wire was subject to direct bending rather than torsional loading (as in the case of a coil) the hairpin spring was more susceptible to any surface defect.

Supplied by George Salter & Co. Ltd. of West Bromwich, the springs closed conventional steel valves, sodium cooled on the exhaust side. The valves seated on bronze-based inserts in the alloy head and were driven by the twin overhead camshafts through short piston-style tappets, with valve clearance effected by means of shims placed in hardened thimbles on the ends of the valve stems.

The camshafts were carried in separate magnesium boxes mounted off the head on pedestals with the hairpin springs thus exposed between head and cambox. The tappets operated through the floor of the cambox and oil was pumped to each cambox with drain pipes to return it to the sump. Seepage down the sides of the tappets was minimal since the tappets were a very precise fit in bronze bushes in the camboxes.

The overhead camshafts ran in plain bearings and were gear driven off the nose of the crankshaft, a train of spur gears working in an oil-tight gear chest at the front of the engine. A gear on the nose of the crankshaft drove each camshaft through three intermediate gears mounted on roller bearings. The upper of two common intermediate gears drove a shaft that projected forward to provide power for the injection pump and magneto. A gear on the front of the short shaft drove a gear above located on the back of the pump and a gear below powering a magneto pulley. The magneto was set below the pump and was driven via a short belt.

The water and oil pumps were situated in a separate casting at the front of the sump and were driven by a second gear on the nose of the crankshaft. The dry sump engine carried a stiff steel crankshaft in its sturdy Rolls Royce derived crankcase. Naturally this continued to run

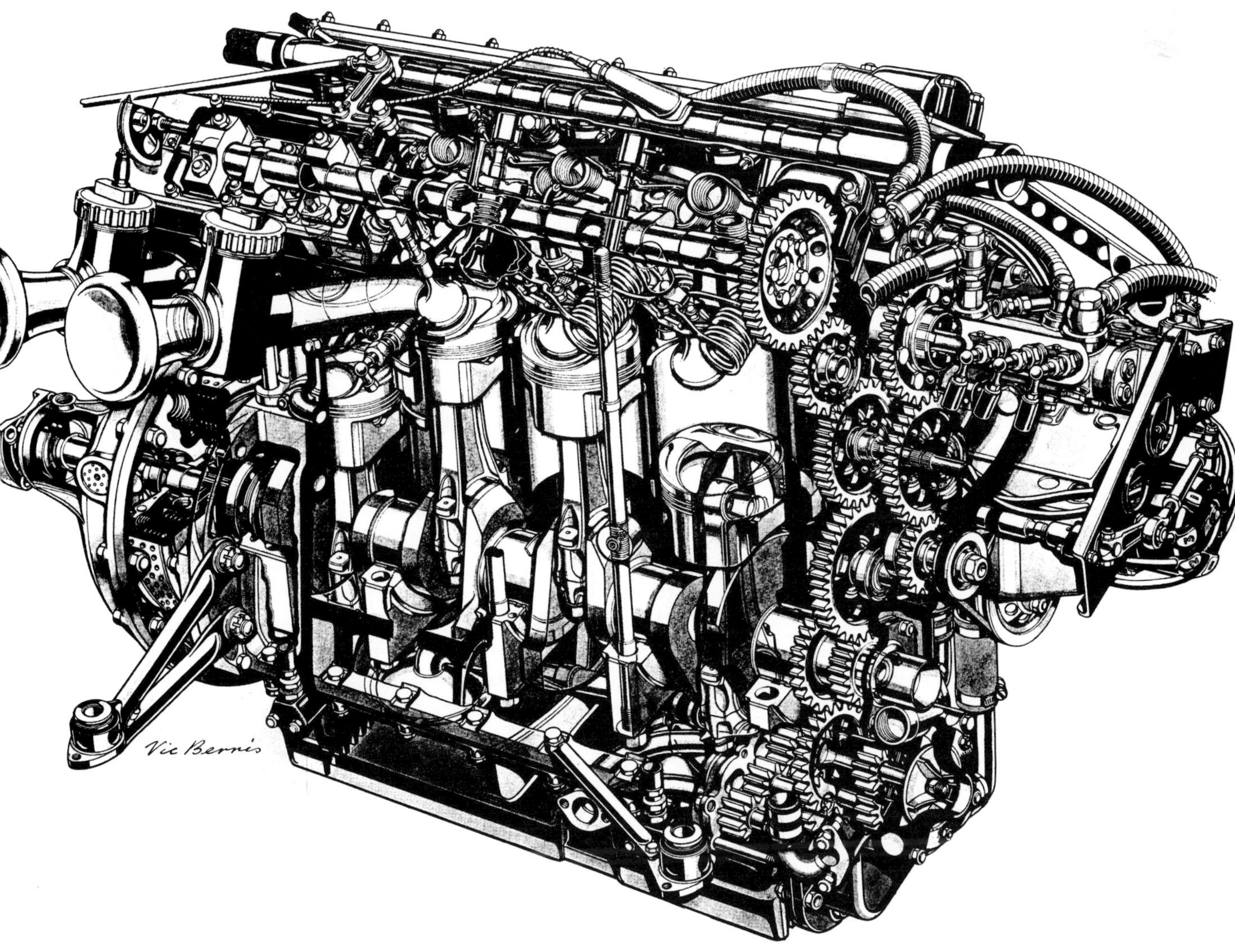

on Vandervell bearings, whereas the dominant Mercedes of '54/'55 had employed roller mains. Roller bearings reduced frictional losses but tended to be less dependable and in '56 the entire field was to be found running on Park Royal's Thinwall bearings.

The crankshaft was forged by the Smith-Clayton Forge, Lincoln in 1% chrome molybdenum steel EN 19 then was sent to Laystall Engineering in Wolverhampton for machining with the final finish for the bearing surfaces done by Vandervell. The 'shaft had a 3.0" centre main bearing, others of 2.75" diameter and 2.4" diameter pins, hence plenty of overlap which together with 0.79" thick webs provided a high level of strength. The crankshaft was driven through two-bolt I-section con rods by Hepworth and Grandage three ring pistons. The con rods were forged from EN24 nickel steel, machined all over and highly polished and carried 1.0" diameter gudgeon pins.

Whereas the original Vanwall engine had its twin plugs fired by a pair of Scintilla magnetos, a double bodied Bosch magneto was now employed, along with the Bosch injection. Still one injector per cylinder injected into the port close to the valve. Connaught had earlier employed indirect injection, on its Formula Two engine and with less success on its 2.5 litre Alta engine. However, it had used the unsophisticated constant flow Hilborn Indy Car system which merely varied the fuel delivery pressure according to engine speed.

The Bosch system employed a multiple-plunger jerk pump, the camshaft of which was geared to run at half engine speed. There was a plunger for each cylinder, operated by its own cam and communicating via high pressure piping with the injector for the appropriate cylinder. Meanwhile, linked to the throttles, a rotating rack and quadrant system turned the plungers in their bores so as to vary the unmasking of plunger control ports which in turn governed the quantity of fuel dispatched to the injector. Thus, the pump - which was mounted on the front of the engine - could respond to engine speed and load (throttle opening in the case of the Vanwall). The injection pressure was no less than 45 bar.

While Connaught's less complex Indy Car technology could work after a fashion thanks to the relative insensitivity of alcohol fuel to mixture strength, it had been found too crude for serious road racing and Connaught had taken its famous Syracuse '55 win after switching to Weber carburettors. Vanwall was alone in deploying fuel injection in 1956.

Following the problems posed by four cylinder engine vibration, the throttle/pump linkage rods had been fitted with Hoffmann control ends. The vibration had been enough to crack the pump mounting flange and Bosch had devised flexible coupling for the drive. Following its withdrawal from racing, Daimler Benz provided information on nozzle sizes and spray angles. Aside from the injection system the main development headaches were exhaust valve and head temperatures and valve spring life.

The head casting had thin walls to allow for the maximum water space and appeared to be distorting at high temperature. Head temperature was critical and a large water temperature gauge had been installed in the cockpit. Springs were undergoing constant development, faced as they were with a total reciprocating weight in the region of 180g. and asked to open the valve fifty times a second at maximum r.p.m. It is also worth noting that piston acceleration was unusually high, this taxing the rings. Piston seizures were not unknown.

For '56 there were revised cam profiles, an improved timing case, rubber rings on the tappets to eliminate oil leakage and refined porting, the latter advised by gas flow expert Harry Weslake. There were also experimental rings and exhaust valves, the latter filled from the top and having a cap rather than the base welded on. This sounds straightforward but involved the use of new equipment by manufacturer Motor Components Ltd. of Birmingham. Both parts were made in austenitic steel with the seating surface stellited. Alas, the prototype broke after 11 hours running.

The V254 engine weighed in at 164kg. complete with clutch, injection and ignition system.

1956 Vanwall 254 engine with Bosch fuel injection and Amal carburettor bodies. Note the cold air box surrounding the trumpets and the neat throttle linkage. This in turn is linked to the Bosch pump which is designed to respond to load as well as engine speed.

Functionally fat

Vandervell multi tubular frame
Unstressed engine
Wishbone front suspension, de Dion rear
Hydraulic dampers
Borrani wire spoke 16" wheels
Vandervell-Goodyear 12" front discs, outboard
Vandervell-Goodyear 11.75" rear discs, inboard
Vandervell-Goodyear two pot calipers
Aluminium bodywork
1 water radiator, 1 oil radiator
Vandervell multi plate clutch
Vandervell five speed gearbox, ZF l.s.d.
35 imp gallon fuel tankage
7' 6.25" wheelbase; 4' 5.75" front track, 4' 3.75" rear.
640kg.

The chassis prepared for the 1956 season were brand new both in terms of structure and aerodynamics.

The structure was the work of Colin Bruce Chapman, successful special builder. Chapman had not discovered circuit racing until 1950 and he had produced his first road racer - an Austin Seven Special - as recently as 1951. Since then he had been a star of the 750 Motor Club's circuit racing arm while steadily developing his Lotus Cars concern.

A Civil Engineer specialist in structures by training, Chapman had immediately grasped that a circuit racing car should have its chassis properly stressed to be functional - that is, to hold all the elements of the car in proper relationship to one another while weighing as little as possible - and that it should keep its wheels as near as possible to vertical while cornering, thereby to develop maximum cornering force. A little negative camber can sometimes be beneficial in this respect but under no circumstances must an outer wheel assume positive camber since that stance significantly reduces grip. Proper wheel control implies a scientifically designed suspension mounted on a rigid chassis.

Chapman had devised complex multi-tubular frames for his early sports racing cars that anticipated the pioneering Formula One solution adopted by Daimler-Benz in 1954, this at a time when the simple ladder frame was the basis of every other Grand Prix car. Still in his mid Twenties, Chapman had moved into small capacity international sports car racing as the German giant set about its conquest of Formula One. Daimler-Benz arrived in its domain with an innovative fully enveloping body, Chapman entered his sphere with an advanced streamlined body. Unveiled for the '54 French Grand Prix, the Mercedes W196 shocked Lotus aerodynamicist Frank Costin by the similarity of its shape to that he had just finalised for Lotus' little sports-racer.

The 1100cc. Costin-bodied Lotus Mark 8 of 1954 featured an advanced chassis frame with riveted aluminium panels adding to the rigidity of a lightweight multi-tubular structure. It also had de Dion rear suspension, swing axle independent front, these systems designed to keep the wheels upright in the corners where rivals' wheels would invariably lean unnervingly, even the outer wheels leaning outwards. The success of the Mark 8 warranted the Costin-inspired approach to Chapman from Vandervell's Grand Prix team: the young constructor was clearly in the forefront of contemporary chassis design.

Chapman was asked to retain the existing Vanwall drivetrain, including proven transaxle, and its front suspension. He could, however, modify this running gear to some extent and he was free to impose his own frame. The existing base was a typical whippy ladder-based tubular affair, the like of which was still employed by Ferrari and the other Italian constructors. Such a frame did not necessarily spoil handling but did not lend itself to soft springing, the use of which could considerably enhance grip - provided it was allied to proper wheel control, which in turn called for chassis rigidity.

Not surprisingly, Chapman's alternative frame was of multi-tubular design, echoing his sports-racers. In other words, it was a practical application of the spaceframe ideal. A spaceframe is so arranged that each component tube is loaded only in tension and compression, never in bending. In practice this requires such complete triangulation of the whole that there can be no provision for a cockpit opening and drivetrain access becomes a nightmare. Chapman arranged for as much triangulation was feasible, designing a lattice work of small diameter tubes in tension or compression and carefully arranged to meet the needs of the existing running gear.

Chapman's suspension alterations included new spring rates in pursuit of the desired softer ride, this to better maintain contact between the tyre and the track. Significantly, the multi-tubular frame Mercedes had enjoyed the softest ride of all '54/'55 Formula One cars.

De Dion rear suspension was universally employed in Formula One following the withdrawal of Daimler-Benz, which had favoured an independent swing axle system. A de Dion system chassis-mounts the heavy transmission components up to and including the differential while universally jointed half shafts feed the wheels which are kept rigidly parallel by a tubular cross-connection. This lateral tube - the heart

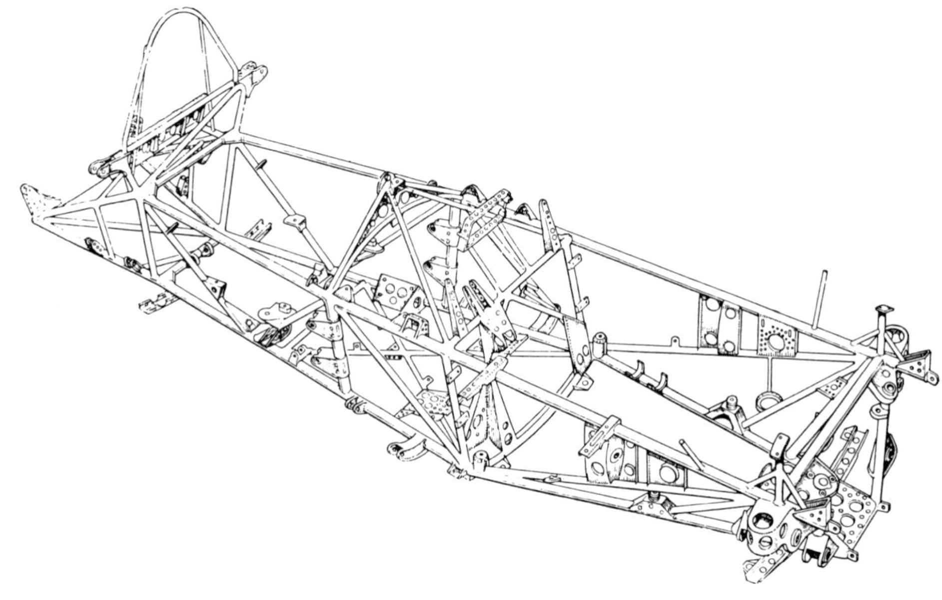

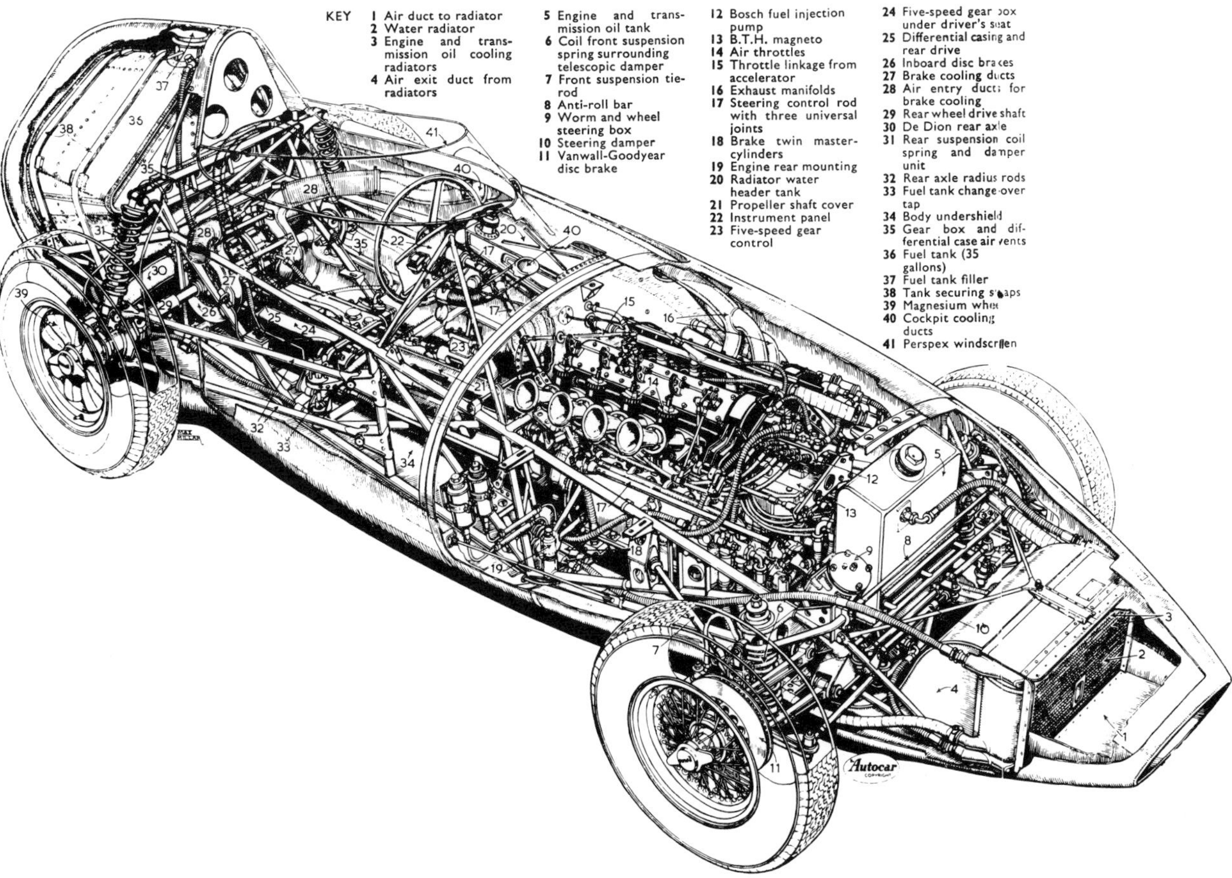

of the system - is free to move up and down and to rock while holding the rear wheels parallel to one another.

Under Chapman the Vanwall's de Dion tube (still working in conjunction with a leaf spring) was properly located via radius rods and a Watts linkage. A Watts linkage pivots the de Dion tube on the centre of a vertical bellcrank, both ends of which are connected to the chassis via ball-jointed horizontal links, these running in opposite directions to meet their respective pick up points. This system allows vertical and rotational movement of the de Dion tube without permitting lateral displacement. With the radius rods, it made for more precise control and avoided unwanted toe-steer.

Other important factors Chapman considered were weight distribution and unsprung weight. To avoid excessive weight in the tail, Chapman went for a three-tank arrangement with saddle tanks either side of the cockpit just ahead of the rear wheels and extending as far forward as the firewall bulkhead. The twin side and single tail tanks were inter-connected and collectively fed a collector pot from which fuel was pumped to the Bosch injection pump. The disadvantage of the side tanks was to make the fuselage fatter, increasing the frontal area of the car.

Clearly, unsprung has to be minimised if soft springing is to be employed to best effect. The Vanwall already had inboard rear brakes and Chapman sought to lighten the de Dion tube, a component which is inherently weighty. Hydraulic telescopic dampers were employed front and rear rather than the traditional rotary vane type in view of the level of suspension movement envisaged. At the front the telescopic dampers neatly and very conveniently fitted inside coil springs.

As we have seen, the retained front suspension was by wishbones while the coils replaced the original Ferrari-inspired leaf springing. The wishbones were parallel and of unequal length, this arrangement offering a low roll centre and, if properly devised, allowing the outer wheel to be kept upright as the car rolls, though with the less heavily loaded inner wheel prone towards positive camber. Chapman paid very careful attention to refinement of the front geometry and he added an anti roll bar, stiffening the front relative to the rear and thus promoting understeer.

The combination of de Dion rear and wishbone and anti roll bar front suspension provided a forward sloping roll axis and this was welcomed in pursuit of understeer, the desired handling characteristic given that in theory the driver could use his excess of power over grip to promote oversteer. Little suspension adjustment was possible at this time, the technique of setting up and driving any of the 2.5 litre cars of the mid Fifties an art rather than a science.

Science was starting to oust art as the main criteria for Formula One bodywork design once more. Picking up the threads of the Thirties, Daimler-Benz had started the ball rolling once more with its fully enveloping shell for the W196. Designed with reference to wind tunnel testing, this reduced drag by a claimed 20% in spite of an inevitable increase in frontal area.

Mercedes' drag reduction was thus achieved through a smoothing of the entire airflow over the car, reducing the effective weight of the turbulent wake that is tugged behind each and every car. Having a fully enveloping body the Mercedes lost the drag penalty promoted by tyre rotation, and also that caused by the interference between the tyres and the fuselage. However, Daimler-Benz soon found it necessary to revert to open wheels, perhaps due to aerodynamic yaw (side acting) effects making the car difficult to drive in fast corners, which it certainly was - witness Fangio struggling at Silverstone in '54.

Meanwhile, Costin's work for Lotus had revolutionised small capacity sports-racing car aerodynamics. Costin had rejected the existing boxy fuselage and cycle wings for a curvaceous all enveloping shell with distinctive tail fins aimed to significantly reduce the drag coefficient. In its Costin bodied form the small Lotus racer found highly impressive speed. Since the car pulled less invisible weight, drag reduction was equivalent to additional horsepower and it went faster.

Clearly, drag was of no less importance given Formula One horsepower and once Chapman's general arrangement drawing was available Costin set about a slippery shape to enclose the Vanwall's revised mechanicals. He devised a tall, fat, long and smooth design with even the underside streamlined. The new look Vanwall was functional rather than beautiful and was notably uncluttered, with a small nose opening and the minimum of other air intakes. The fuselage was somewhat bulbous and a high windscreen blended into a lofty tail leaving the driver completely surrounded by coachwork. Even the exhaust manifold was set into a recess in the scuttle so as not to interrupt the airflow while the surprisingly plump bodyshape was carried very close to the wheels.

Costin's task had in no way been facilitated by the Vanwall's tall engine, high seating position - the driver was perched above the big transmission lump - and Chapman's side tanks. The distinctive new shape had taken five and a half weeks of his spare time, mainly "slide rule pushing". It had been devised purely by mathematics with no reference to wind tunnel testing. There was no styling, and Costin admits he found it difficult to envisage the moulding of a shape in three dimensions as a sculptor might. He worked from aircraft-proven aerodynamic theory.

The three dimensional form that has the lowest drag co-efficient of all in free air is that of a tear drop. In effect, Costin produced a tear drop shape fuselage onto which a smaller tear drop cockpit superstructure was superimposed. The fuselage form was plotted via vertical and horizontal sections taken at regular intervals, front to back and top to bottom, just as a functional ship or aircraft form is devised.

Of course, imposition of the perfect tear drop form was impractical given the constraints posed by the mechanicals. Thus, in cross section the plots were not circular but were elliptical, the resultant effect that of a slightly squashed tear drop, for practical reasons the underside squashed a little more than the topside. The base of the car had to be flat to avoid the need for excessive ride height (and to keep the centre of gravity low) but its lower flanks were well rounded.

Through the length of the car, vertical sections were plotted at five inch intervals. Each quarter ellipse was painstakingly calculated according to its position relative to the front of the car. At the rear, a full length tear drop tail would have added excessive length and weight and thus the overall effect was that of a slightly squashed and truncated tear drop.

Upon close investigation it could be noted in side elevation that Costin had superimposed a reflex curve onto his main tear drop form. A reflex aerofoil has a conventional aerofoil front and centre section - the former sweeping up, the latter down - followed by an additional upsweep at the rear, lifting its trailing edge. The reflex aerofoil has a stable centre of pressure, unlike the conventional aerofoil and it was this stability that Costin sought.

In itself, the tear drop shape does not generate lift, merely a pitching moment which tries to lift the nose as power is applied. A similar pitching effect can be caused by air packing underneath the nose in the case of a car. A combination of high power, soft suspension and a heavy rear fuel load could all further contribute to the unwanted rearward pitch of a Fifties Grand Prix car under acceleration. The reflex form countered this tendency via basic aerodynamics.

The fuselage had to be fat at the firewall bulkhead, due to the need to accommodate the side tanks and given reasonable track dimensions it then came unavoidably close to the front and rear wheels. Costin did not consider interference from wheel rotation would significantly affect the overall airflow due to the narrowness of the wheels causing minimal turbulence. The wheels were not considered part of the overall streamlined form, rather they were an unavoidable nuisance. Ideally, the car would have had enclosed wheels but this would have added weight and have made servicing more difficult, and would have posed tyre and brake cooling difficulties.

The fuselage sides had to be scalloped out between the front wheels to allow for wheel movement. Air flowing inside the front wheels tended to separate from the body but naturally re-attached itself to the bulging flanks either side of the engine bay. Air separated again just ahead of the rear wheels and the flow was then lost but above the wheels the flow stayed attached much further back, over the tail.

Costin's overall aim was to keep the airflow attached to the fuselage for as long as was possible since it is when airflow detaches that drag inducing turbulence is created, adding to the size and hence weight of the invisible drogue towed behind the car. Air is keen to flow from high to low pressure but is reluctant to go in the other direction, thus Costin avoided any unnecessary protrusion, minimising pressure build-up points.

Better fat and able to keep air attached than slim with protrusions. Overall drag is a product of the non dimensional drag co-efficient and frontal area and for the Vanwall the co-efficient was all important. In other words, the overall shaping of the car for the minimisation of its turbulent wake was more important than piecemeal reduction of its frontal area which was unavoidably high in any case.

Of course, unlike an aeroplane, Costin's Vanwall fuselage was not designed to run in free air but in close proximity to the ground. The ground is still, the undertray of the car is moving and this creates friction which manifests itself as swirling vortices. The modified-tear drop fuselage's curved belly flanks provided a smooth escape route for these vortices. Further, the fact that the undertray was upswept towards the rear recognised that this ground shear effect increases towards the rear.

Projecting above the main fuselage, the driver's head and shoulders were fully faired in via the aforementioned superimposed tear drop shape superstructure. Again this had to be of modified tear drop form. It was pure tear drop in plan but had a high back, over the rear tank. Since the cockpit did not have a roof air broke loose behind the wrap-around windscreen - which was as high as was practical - and the high back encouraged it to reattach itself to the bodywork, delaying final separation.

Where the superstructure joined the main fuselage there was an expanding fillet to control turbulence, just as can be seen forming the joint between a Spitfire wing and fuselage. Thus, air was persuaded that it wanted to stay attached to body all the way back to the rear tank, aside that is from the lower portion flowing over the flanks and meeting rear wheel interference.

At the front of the fuselage was a small nose intake, this feeding a radiator system that took care of all the car's water and oil cooling requirements. Unusually, Costin provided both an inlet and an outlet for the cooling air flow, the outlet set between the front wheels underneath the car. At that point there was low pressure due to the effect of air squeezing, hence accelerating between the front wheels. Thus, the radiator flow was the opposite of a venturi, air expanding and thus slowing and gaining pressure ahead of the radiator then, heated, rushing out the other side to join the underbody low pressure area.

For the engine air intake Costin rejected a pitot-style ram air intake, reasoning that the potential gain in engine performance was not worth the implicit loss of aerodynamic performance (through additional turbulence). Thus, he looked to a flush intake and specified the NACA duct, well established in the aircraft world but unknown in car racing. The suction of the engine trumpets was enough to activate the drag-free NACA duct but it was not 100% efficient in its operation since there was static pressure above it. For 100% efficiency the pressures above and below a NACA duct have to be the same.

The exhaust pipe was another lump that Costin faired in as much as was possible to minimise turbulence. While he was able to sink the forward potion to the level of the bodywork, the tail pipe had to stay proud of the rear tank: since it was further back it did less damage in terms of air flow disruption. Rear view mirrors alongside the cockpit were unavoidable protrusions so Costin cleverly incorporated cockpit cooling air scoops in them.

Equally as clever was Costin's method of cooling the inboard rear brakes. Where air broke away just ahead of the rear wheels there was a local area of static pressure. Inside the cockpit air was at low pressure, thus a hole cut in the side of the fuselage at the point of static air saw air rush in the cockpit. Costin arranged for air to rush in via a system of ducting which took it over the rear brakes. In fact, behind the axle the disc ran in a cold air box - not unlike a giant empty caliper - which was sealed to it via a knife-edge scraper each side. The cold air was piped in from the opening in the side of the fuselage and was expelled from the box through the cockpit, the brake dust it picked up en route soon blackening the driver's face!

Overall, in frontal area the Vanwall was now over 10% greater than the rival Maserati 250F thanks to the large faired side tanks and tail but Costin knew it had a significantly lower coefficient of drag. The precise measure was unknown since there had been no wind tunnel investigation. Skin friction drag tends to be significant in terms of the last two or three m.p.h. and thus marginally influences speed at Rheims, if not at Monte Carlo. Nevertheless, the Vanwall was always presented with a body polished until it was like glass.

Aside from frame, suspension and aerodynamics, the other major change from the '55 specification chassis was in modification of the gearbox, which was redesigned to accept an additional gear (providing five speeds plus reverse). With five speeds, first was only required for starting and the top four were fitted with Porsche-patent synchromesh in a new deal with Porsche of Stuttgart. The gearbox was fed oil from the main engine supply at reduced pressure. Its sump was well baffled minimising aeration and consequently it enjoyed good clean and cool oil. Oil was squirted at each gear to assist cooling.

The gearbox was in unit with the final drive and was fed via a Vandervell multi-plate clutch. The gearbox ratios were fixed, with variations to suit different tracks possible via optional final drive ratios. The fixed ratios, from top were 1.0, 1.12, 1.40, 1.96 and 2.80 while the variable final drive ratios were from 3.27 to 6.06.

Final drive was through a conventional ZF limited slip differential while the half shafts were equipped with universal joints to accommodate the vertical movement of the wheels relative to the transaxle. It was therefore necessary to allow for variations in shaft length and each shaft was split into male and female parts with a sliding splined joint passing the drive. Unusually, a ball spline was employed, this having rows of steel balls to separate driving and driven faces, the intention being to avoid 'stiction' which could inhibit suspension movement.

At the front the Vanwall employed forged

wishbones and kingpins and coil springs over dampers worked by the forward leg of the lower wishbone. Chapman's anti roll bar connected the upper wishbones, from which radius arms ran back to frame. The well triangulated frame extended from front suspension mounts to rear suspension mounts with a combined oil and water radiator outrigged ahead, the 35 gallon fuel tankage attached behind and to its flanks.

The small diameter tube frame weighed approximately 90 lbs and had prominent pyramid bracing at the central scuttle. The engine extended ahead of this, the prop shaft behind and below the cockpit floor and feeding the transmission assembly set under the driver's seat. The rear fuel tank took up all the space in the tail while an aluminium oil tank serving both engine and transmission was set immediately ahead of the engine, between the front suspension coils.

The fuel tanks were made in Italy of riveted aluminium by Salamino Ildebrando of Parma using the de Bergue system of riveting developed for aircraft tanks. In '55 Vanwall had tried rubber cell-equipped aircraft tanks but the cells had leaked in the face of the fuel employed.

The radiator header tank was set conveniently upon the scuttle pyramid. The radiator incorporated matrixes for oil and water cooling. The well polished body was of aluminium and was secured by flush fitting, aircraft style Dzus fasteners. It was 14 feet long while the car stood 3 3/4 feet high. The driver sat behind a perspex windshield and found a left handed gearchange in an open gate.

Steering was via a worm and wheel system while braking was still the impressive Vandervell-Goodyear system, only BRM and Connaught likewise employing disc systems. The Vanwall system was notable for its radial disc ventilation and its hinged calipers. The front discs were of 12" diameter and were hub mounted while the rear discs flanking the transmission were of 11.75" diameter. Lockheed twin master cylinders and pipework were employed.

The Vanwall ran on Borrani 16" wire spoke rim wheels of the Rudge Whitworth centre lock pattern and having lightweight alloy rims and knock off hub caps. Pirelli natural rubber tread, cotton carcase crossply tyres were standard wear, the fronts of 5.50" section, the rears of 7.00".

DIARY

Park Royal (GB) January 22

The Vanwall team made no attempt to contest the Argentine Grand Prix which opened the 1956 World Championship season at Buenos Aires. In its absence Ferrari fought Maserati, private examples of the red cars swelling the grid to 13 entries. Taking over Luigi Musso's car, Juan Manuel Fangio was a convincing victor in the latest Maranello-modified version of the Lancia D.50.

Silverstone (GB) May 5
International Trophy
Moss .... Q: 1/R:1
Schell .... Q: 2/R:NR

Vandervell made the International Trophy an exception to his rule of contesting only World Championship events and Maserati Team Leader Stirling Moss agreed to sample the new Green challenger, joining Harry Schell. BRM, Connaught and Ferrari comprised the factory opposition for the event which was run over 180 miles - 60% of Grand Prix distance. Both Vanwalls lined up on the front row of the grid ahead of Fangio's Ferrari modified Lancia and Mike Hawthorn's lone BRM, while the second Ferrari of Peter Collins and Roy Salvadori's private Maserati were also under the three year old circuit record set up by Farina in the Thinwall Special.

Fangio made the best start but Hawthorn came through to lead the first lap, ahead of the World Champion and the Vanwalls. Schell overtook Moss but after a couple of laps Moss was ahead again and on lap six of 60 he displaced Fangio. Meanwhile Hawthorn was leading in convincing style having set a new lap record. The two British cars steadily dropped the Lancia-Ferrari and on lap 14 Moss inherited the lead as Hawthorn coasted to a halt with a sheared magneto drive. Meanwhile Schell had fallen behind Collins and, following a stop to change plugs, at one third distance he pitted with terminal trouble: a broken fuel injector pipe. On lap 21 Collins was called in to hand over to Fangio, who had met clutch trouble. No sooner had Fangio gotback up to speed than the malady struck for a second time. Moss was left completely unchallenged yet he went on to win at an average speed slightly in excess of Farina's old lap record, equaling Hawthorn's new lap record 14 times. The second placed Connaught was a lap adrift.

Monte Carlo (MON) May 13
Monaco Grand Prix
Schell .... Q: 5/R:NR
Trintignant ...... Q: 6/R:NR

Full engagement: Moss back at Maserati, supported by Jean Behra and Cesare Perdisa; Fangio heading the Ferrari challenge supported by Eugenio Castellotti, Collins and Musso. Gordini represented France with three cars while Vanwall and BRM represented Great Britain with two cars apiece, Maurice Trintignant joining Schell. BRM was well off the pace and had to withdraw following valve problems in practice.

With a couple of 250F privateers in the fray, that left 14 cars on the three-two-three grid. The Vanwalls had made a splendid practice showing with the cars sharing fifth fastest time, just 1.6 seconds slower than pole man Fangio.

Moss jumped into an immediate lead over the Lancia-Ferraris of Fangio and Castellotti with Schell fourth, Trintignant thirteenth, nose damage telling of a tangle with another car at the first corner. The same corner saw Fangio spin on the second lap and Schell was unable to avoid him, the Vanwall spearing into the straw bales. At the end of the fifth lap Trintignant joined him on the sidelines, his nos damage having caused engine overhea ing.

Moss' 250F led the race start to finis

Spa Francorchamps (B) June 3
Belgian Grand Prix
Schell .... Q: 6/R: 4
Trintignant ...... Q: 7/R: NR

The Francorchamps action commence on the Thursday with Moss and Fang trading fastest lap, the Lancia-Ferra ending up quickest at 249.8 seconds. Th Vanwalls did not arrive until the Frida when the track was wet but on Saturda Schell cut a 259 second lap. He was 4 thus slower than poleman Fangio, where at Monte Carlo he had been 1.5% slowe Second on the grid, Moss had a rebodie high cockpit coaming Maserati clear inspired by the new Vanwall shap Maserati ran its regular trio while Ferra replaced Musso by Paul Frere and loane a fifth example to local Gordini driv Andre Pilette. Gordini was absent, as w the troubled BRM team.

Moss led from the start chased by th three quickest Lancia-Ferraris and Behra 250F while Schell lay sixth, Trintigna seventh. By the end of the first lap bot British cars had demoted Behra. By th fifth lap Fangio had moved into the lea and Trintignant had made a quick sto while Schell had likewise fallen behin Behra and Frere. Trintignant was soon i again to further investigate the cause lost power and he fell out after 10 laps, th culprit a broken fuel line. Meanwhil Schell had settled down to follow Fre home, "driving the Vanwall with discre tion", according to The Autocar. He fe well back from Frere who was the on driver to run the full distance withou trouble, aside from winner Collin However, having suffered a broken hu Moss was able to take over Perdisa's ca and claw back onto the lead lap, leavin

Diary continues on page 38

Too Much Shake

Vandervell was a man to let his results do the talking. The International Trophy win against the new combination of World Champion Fangio and the Lancia-Ferrari told British enthusiasts that at last the country had a car capable of taking the fight to the Italians. Alas, the expectations aroused by Silverstone were found to have been somewhat premature. Without Moss the Vanwall team was a sometimes a threat, never a natural leader. The revised car's pace was inconsistent and reliability was still lacking.

Schell did a spirited job but he was not an Ace and while his approach did much to encourage the team he was incapable of showing the full potential of the big green machine. This season Fangio and Moss were the Aces; Collins, Hawthorn, Musso and Castellotti formed the next rank. BRM had done well to secure Hawthorn's services but it did not manage to keep him fully in contention and towards the end of the season the Englishman went back to Maranello.

Clearly the Vanwall's strong suit was its aerodynamics: both at Rheims and at Monza Schell came through to join battle for the lead. On the other hand high speed handling was not its forte, as witness Spa Francorchamps where Schell could pass the Italian cars on top speed on the Masta straight only to lose out through the somewhat bumpy Stavelot sweep. The car absorbed the bumps well but Schell lacked the cornering speed of the Italian machines. He finished the Belgian Grand Prix fourth a lap down. And that was the only one of the five World Championship races he finished without major delay. Indeed, his delayed tenth at Rheims was the only other finish of 12 Grand Prix starts for the team.

On the positive side, it was clear that the Vanwall was an advanced design with a powerful engine which lacked only high speed handling finesse - it was very competitive at the slow Monte Carlo circuit - and the eradication of the persistent gremlins. There was no fundamental mechanical flaw in its design. The only alterations to the basic specification made during the season were a switch to a stronger de Dion tube for Monza (in view of the stresses imposed by the banking) and (after the British Grand Prix) the introduction of a modified crankcase with a larger front main bearing, plus modified c.v. joints and fuel tanks in the light of the failures in the Silverstone race.

The fuel tank modification followed the discovery that the fuel filters had become clogged with a residue that was eventually traced to a silicate used to seal the tank. The ageing of this material did not worry the Italian cars - which used the same tank supplier - since Weber carburation required less sensitive filtering.

Of the ten Grand Prix race retirements, Silverstone accounted for three, the shunts at Monaco for two, suspension failures at Monza for two more, then there were a gearbox oil leak for Schell at Monza and two injection system failures, for Trintignant at Francorchamps and Schell at Rheims. A third injection system failure sidelined Schell during the International Trophy. At Silverstone and Francorchamps an injection pipe broke, at Rheims the control linkage broke. These failures were all related to the vibration of the four cylinder engine.

Engine reliability was much better this season. Of course, valves and valve springs were the subject of on-going development for reliability and this season, at the suggestion of Daimler Benz German spring manufacturer S. Scherdel KG supplied springs of chrome vandium to EN50. Further, German piston manufacturer Mahle supplied a piston of a slightly different alloy that was heavier - by 16 grammes - but

Diary continued

Schell's lapped Vanwall fourth.

Rheims (F) July 1
French Grand Prix
Schell .... Q: 4/R:NR
Hawthorn ....Q: 6/R:10 (Schell)
Chapman .... Q: 5/Withdrew

The BRM team absent once again, Hawthorn joined the Vanwall squad for the ultra-fast Rheims circuit and in practice he won the 100 bottles of champagne on offer for the first driver to break the 200 k.p.h. barrier. Hawthorn was replacing Trintignant and both he and Schell outran the Maserati force (Moss in the rebodied car backed by Behra, Perdisa and Piero Taruffi), if not the Ferrari squad. The Vanwall drivers lined up behind Fangio, Castellotti and Collins who had used modified, bigger bore Lancia V8 engines to secure the front row.

Maranello sent five cars in all while Gordini with three cars and a new Bugatti project carried the hopes of France. Vanwall had made a surprise third entry of Colin Chapman but he had to stand down following a practice incident. During the second session Chapman had found a rear brake lock, the pad welding itself to the disc, and he had hit the rear of Hawthorn's sister car. As a consequence Vanwall could field only two race cars, a great shame since Chapman had joined the select band of six drivers over 200k.p.h.

On race afternoon Hawthorn was suffering from having driven the 12 Hour sports car race overnight. First time around, the front row cars led Schell and Hawthorn with Moss sixth. Schell dropped back on the second lap, suffering fuel injection trouble which led to his retirement after only six laps. Since Hawthorn was feeling unwell Schell took over his car after 11 of the 61 laps, rejoining seventh as Moss stopped with a broken gear lever. By lap twenty he was fifth and a lap later de Portago's Lancia- Ferrari fell out, leaving the Vanwall a clear road to the three front row cars.

Significantly, Schell had been catching the leaders at the rate of up to five seconds per lap. He was with them by half distance and he completed lap 31 second to Fangio. Collins and Castellotti had been advised by the Ferrari team that the Vanwall was a lap adrift! For three laps Schell challenged the World Champion, drawing alongside on the long Thillois straight, then his heavily stressed engine lost its edge. A couple of circumspect tours, then the Vanwall was in for pits attention and it limped home tenth, five laps down. Fangio was also delayed by a pit stop and Collins beat Castellotti by a head with Behra's Maserati third.

Silverstone (GB) July 14
British Grand Prix
Schell............. Q: 5/R:NR
Trintignant...... Q:16/R:NR
Gonzalez......... Q: 6/R:NR

Hawthorn was back in a BRM at Silverstone and he headed the British car challenge, joining poleman Moss and Fangio on the front row. The Vanwall team again wheeled out a third car, this time for '51 and '54 Silverstone winner Jose Froilan Gonzalez. The Argentinian had in the past driven Vandervell's Thinwall Special. However, he and Schell could but match the practice time of Salvadori's privately run 250F which was fourth quickest while returnee Trintignant languished further back. As usual, Maserati ran three works cars while BRM matched that and Ferrari fielded four cars. With private Maseratis, two works Gordinis, three Connaughts and British hopefuls Emeryson and Bristol-Cooper the field was 27-strong.

Hawthorn led from the flag, chased by Fangio, Brooks, Schell and Salvadori as Gonzalez was left stationary, victim of broken half shaft. By the end of the fir lap Fangio had fallen back, leaving th two BRMs ahead of Schell but this time was Vanwall rather than BRM which fa tered at Silverstone, Schell losing plac before stopping to have a damper re placed. Then there was more trouble i the form of fuel starvation brought abo by filters clogging with aluminium du from the fuel tank.

This trouble, as the potent fuel in us this weekend attacked the metal of th tank, affected both cars and brought abou a number of stops before they finally re tired. Trintignant had earlier replaced magneto lead. Meanwhile, Fangio ha come up to split the leading BRMs only t spin, then Moss had fought his way throug to the front. The BRM challenge had sub sequently fizzled out. Moss found troubl and Fangio eventually won.

Park Royal (GB) August 5

Disheartened, Vandervell kept his troub led cars in London rather than contest th punishing German Grand Prix over th taxing 14 mile Nurburgring mountai circuit. BRM also avoided the race an Ferrari had a clear edge over Maserat Fangio taking a straightforward win.

Monza (I) September 2
Italian Grand Prix
Schell Q:10/R:NR
Trintignant...... Q:11/R:NR
Taruffi .... Q: 4/R:NR

The World Championship finale was hel over Monza Park's 6.24 mile (10.04km. combined road and banked circuit, th high speed banking notoriously bumpy Vanwall sent over three cars - the third fo Italian Piero Taruffi - to meet four work 250Fs and six Lancia- Ferraris with Gordin and Connaught also represented, by thre cars apiece. Two of the Maseratis were

Diary continues on page 40

ctory first time for Moss in the nwall! This is ex-Mercedes ver in the 1956 ernational Trophy, debut race for the stin/Chapman re-ed car. Moss ished one lap ahead the rest of the ld, raising British pes for Vanwall's rand Prix perform-ce.

could better withstand heat and offered lower friction. Mahle pistons were in Taruffi's car at Monza.

At Monza the Vanwall reached a speed in the region of 165m.p.h. On the basis of a power output of 280b.h.p. a top speed of 165m.p.h. and a frontal area of 12.8 square feet, Costin calculates drag of 500lbs. and a drag co-efficient of Cd Ç 0.585. The car did not demonstrate significant body lift at high speed, perhaps 1.0" and due mainly to the effect of air packing underneath. It was clearly more 'slippery' than any rival.

Significantly, no modification was required to Costin's original aerodynamic prescription (though the brake cooling was sometimes over-effective, leading to the intake holes being partially blanked off). Trintignant was shorter than Schell and at Monte Carlo he complained that the wrap-around screen spoiled his view of the corners but it was not practical to substitute an aero screen. Right to the end of the season the car ran as it had first turned out at Goodwood in mid March, with Guy Anthony Vandervell at the controls. During that first test Costin had carried out some tufting tests which had confirmed his book work.

The experience of the first full season emphasised that Costin had got the aerodynamics right while the car's dry weight was measured as 1346lb. which compares well to that of the front running Italian cars. Engine performance was not lacking and, aside from enhanced reliability, the main challenge was suspension development. Remember that there are many variables to play with (tyre pressures, dampers, springs, roll bars, caster and camber and so forth) and with the benefit of a season's hindsight Formula One newcomer Chapman was able to make some important refinements to his package to enhance the grip and handling for '57.

It was obvious that Vandervell had the basis of a consistent Grand Prix winner and that gave Maserati and Ferrari cause for a certain amount of anxiety. A substantial threat from Britain was something entirely new to them.

Not that the BRM team was to be discounted: at Silverstone for both the International Trophy and the Grand Prix it showed very well in the talented hands of Hawthorn and Brooks. Indeed, Hawthorn might well have stolen Moss'

Diary continued

new cars with offset seat and angled prop shaft allowing the driver to sit very low for a significant reduction of frontal area. However, Ferrari dominated practice, Castellotti and Musso joining Fangio on the front row. Next up was Taruffi, ahead of both offset 250Fs. Castellotti and Musso ran off at the start, setting an imprudent pace: tyre failures cost their chances after only four of 50 laps. That left the leaders as Fangio, Moss, Collins, Taruffi and Schell who had come through quickly from the fourth row. The leaders were in a slip-streaming bunch, Schell had already run ahead of Fangio and soon Fangio, Moss and Schell broke away. On lap nine Schell took the lead emporarily from Moss' off-set car, then Taruffi stopped from fifth position.

Lap ten saw Fangio leading Moss and Schell, next time around Schell was in the lead. Moss then regained the advantage. Moss and Schell could pull away from Fangio on the banking but the Lancia caught up again on the road section. Shortly before half distance Fangio retired, then on lap 27 Schell pitted, dropping to fourth. He completed only four more laps before succumbing to transmission failure. Earlier, both Taruffi and Trintignant had succumbed to suspension failure. Moss eventually won while Fangio was forced to take over Collins' car to collect second and the World Championship crown.

24

International Trophy glory had not the BRM failed him.

The four cylinder BRM was small, light and very powerful. But this season BRM fortunes sank from bad to worse. It started with Hawthorn's car suffering transmission failure at Goodwood, skidding off the track and turning over, thankfully without injury to its driver. Then Hawthorn went out at Aintree with brake failure, happily with less spectacular consequences. Then in practice for the International Trophy he was clouted in the face by his bonnet...

At Silverstone Hawthorn set a fastest lap prior to his departure with engine failure that Moss was able to equal 14 times but was unable to improve upon. The two four cylinder British cars looked well matched. Then the Bourne challenger had to be withdrawn from the Monaco Grand Prix due to distorted inlet valves, a problem that kept the team from the Belgian and French Grands Prix. Back at Silverstone, the BRM was the fastest car in the race, Hawthorn clocking 137.4m.p.h. on the Hanger Straight while Schell was next up at 136.8m.p.h.

Both British cars had a speed advantage over the Italian machines. The fact that the BRM could match Vanwall speed with a body shape that was clearly less aerodynamic suggests that either it had more power or that it was getting onto the Hanger straight faster. The speeds recorded at Silverstone were 30m.p.h. down on those seen at Rheims where the succession of drops in the long, long straight helped a car show its absolute flat out potential.

BRM's Silverstone pace was to no avail: Hawthorn's transmission seized and Brooks suffered a sticking throttle, the upshot of which was that he hit a bank, writing off his car and breaking his jaw. BRM withdrew for the remainder of the season. Mays reported: "Hawthorn and Brooks felt they had had enough of the car... The year had been as black and disastrous as any we had experienced with the sixteen-cylinder car".

Brooks later tested the car again, setting promising times at Monza. However, the rising star

Rheims 1956 wa memorable race British enthusia Schell taking Vanwall into the l of the French Gra Prix. On the pre ous spread he is p tured closing on leading Ferrari t which had assum he was a lap dou But the Vanu driver was enjoy the benefit of sup aerodynamics a excellent brake

ell at Spa Fran-
hamps, ahead of
Lancia-Ferrari of
lins. The Vanwall
er had a trouble-
race but lacked
e, finishing
th a lap down.
British car was
yet ready to
w its driver to
le the high speed
eps of the Belgian
uit with his char-
ristic gusto.

declined to stay with the team, leaving the way open for him to move to Vanwall, which was meanwhile testing in England with Moss. Though its car was fast, Moss did not see potential in the unhappy BRM operation for his '57 challenge. The troubles facing BRM helped paved the way for Vandervell to put together an all-British team for '57 that was capable of building on the Vanwall's obvious promise.

The withdrawal of Daimler-Benz had left Grand Prix racing more open, though primarily red at the front as Vanwall and BRM struggled and Connaught and Gordini failed to make a mark. For Connaught and Gordini shortage of finance and lack of engine power was telling. Meanwhile, neither the works Maserati team led by Moss nor the works Ferrari team led by Fangio could claim supremacy. The advantage swung back and forth.

In '55 the Lancia D.50 had looked to be superior to the Maserati 250F but though its engine appeared stronger this season, it was by no means a more competitive car. Following the introduction of an over-square version of the Lancia V8 at Rheims, Ferrari claimed 275b.h.p. at 8,000r.p.m. Meanwhile, chassis modifications had been intended to mitigate the cornering power of the rear tyres and thereby make the low polar moment of inertia machine more driveable.

Whereas the original Lancia had carried its fuel in pannier tanks between the wheels, Ferrari relocated the bulk of the load in the tail. The panniers themselves were blended into the body where previously they had been outrigged. The entire philosophy of the advanced machine was altered, to make it more conventional and more manageable. Meanwhile, the switch to Engelbert tyres had put Ferrari at something of a disadvantage compared to the Pirelli runners.

Only narrowly defeated in the title chase, Maserati had continued to hone its established 250F design. The in line six engine received slight modification to its combustion chamber shape and power was reputedly 270b.h.p. at 8,000r.p.m. A Vanwall inspired high cockpit coaming was introduced at Francorchamps yet neither in Belgium nor in France could Moss

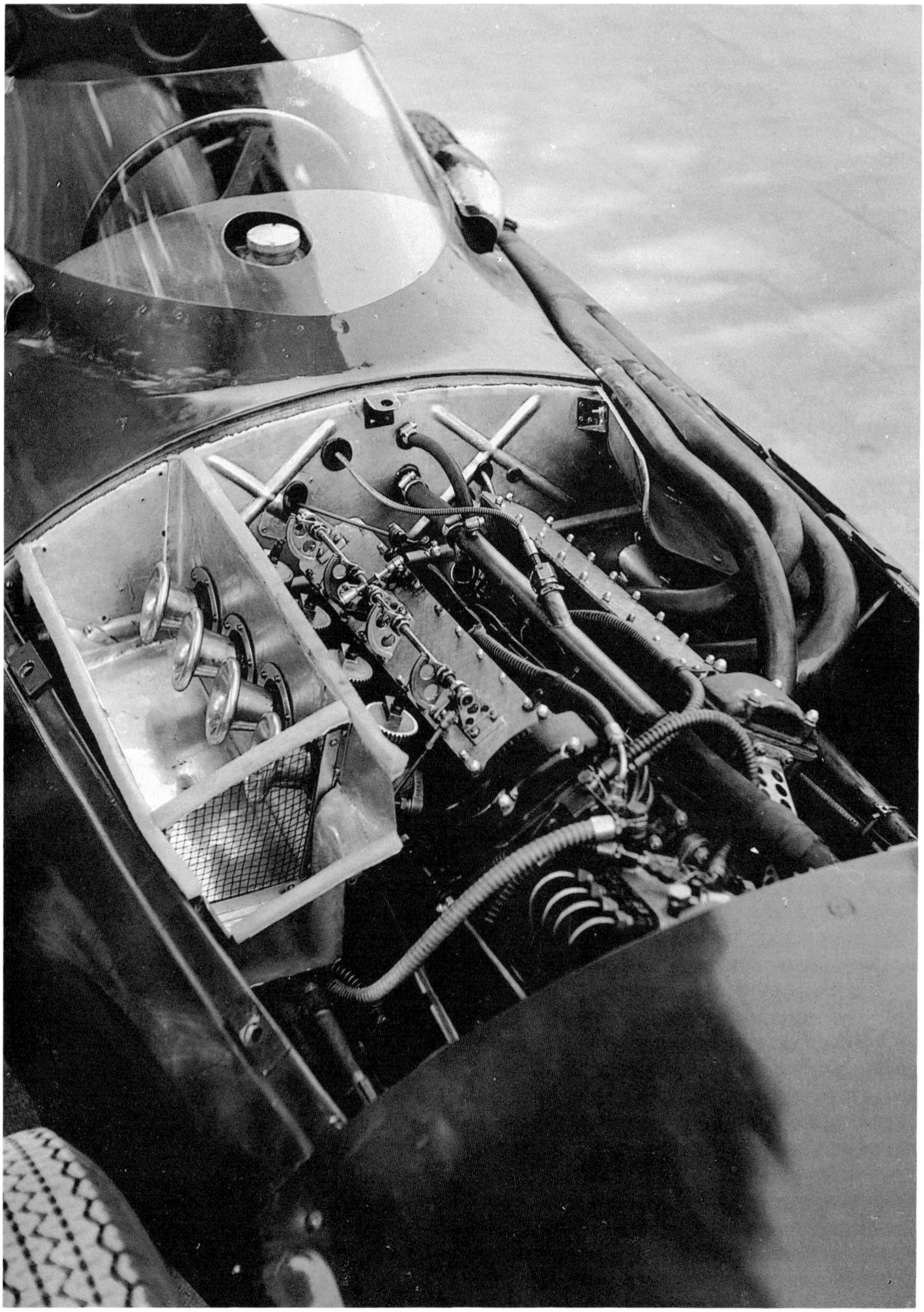

Fuel injected engi
pictured at Mor
Carlo in 195

wall cockpit
ils showing
rchange (top) and
ith the seat re-
ed - the final
e unit over which
driver was
ched.

challenge Fangio in the dry.

In '55 Maserati had toyed with a fully enveloping body but this had not been a success. Instead for Monza the marque looked to a reduced frontal area, building a pair of brand new chassis with the prop shaft offset alongside the driver through an angling of the engine and a revised transmission. This allowed the driver to sit lower in the car and offered the additional benefit of lowering the centre of gravity. The bodywork was duly revised, lower and sleeker, the car much lower than the Vanwall, to which it had a comparable top speed.

Other less significant developments by Maserati this season were disc brakes and fuel injection, neither of which Ferrari considered worthwhile. Maserati found the distance between Modena and the UK a major handicap in its deployment of discs, while there proved to be insufficient gain to prompt it to tackle the problem avidly. Thus, only the British and French cars raced discs, even though, with competition closer there was more emphasis upon braking than ever according to Fangio.

Maserati was the only rival team to try fuel injection this season. First Maserati tried its own version of the Bosch high pressure indirect system as used by Vanwall, producing an engine with marginally higher top end power but too steep a power curve. Next came a direct injection engine which proved more driveable but too heavy on fuel. Neither avenue of development led anywhere.

Meanwhile, running on carburettors, the BRM in line four was at least as powerful as the injected Vanwall engine, injection promoting driveability rather than power for the latter. The BRM engine had a significantly larger bore than its Park Royal rival, displacing 102.87 x 74.93mm. It was run to well over 8,000r.p.m. though officially it produced 270b.h.p. at 7,500r.p.m. The big bore engine had very large inlet valves for maximum top end power and these were the root of the problem that manifested itself at Monte Carlo.

The BRM reappeared at Silverstone with a modified valve that of necessity had a flat rather than concave head. This had the effect of increasing the compression ratio and forced a reduced maximum engine speed but this was still as high as 8,000r.p.m. and no significant power loss was evident.

The BRM was the smallest and lightest of the serious runners in '56, and with Connaught the only one to run a four speed gearbox. All contenders other than Gordini ran a de Dion rear suspension and Vanwall arguably had the most advanced chassis with its complex multi-tubular frame. However, as we have noted, it did not have a handling advantage. The best handling car of '56 was the extremely well balanced 250F, the performance of the Lancia-Ferrari spoiled somewhat by its unconventional tyres.

Pirelli supplied 17" rim tyres for Monza in view of the banking and Vanwall and Maserati were free from tyre troubles. However, Ferrari had to be more careful with its Engelbert covers. Fangio warned Musso and Castellotti that fresh tyres had to be nursed on a full fuel load otherwise centrifugal force might throw the tread off. That warning went unheeded...

Overall, then, a season of mixed fortune for all the leading contenders. The Autocar commented of the more open competition: "this undoubtedly reflects the amount of finance available. It is impossible to obtain facts in this matter but without question Daimler-Benz was able to invest astronomical sums in its racing programme... The vital factor in top racing is to be able to redesign, prove and produce new parts for all cars quickly when a defect is discovered; this requires very large resources".

Vandervell had the resources to match those available to the Italian teams. British enthusiasts awaited 1957 with justifiably high expectations.

Vanwall upright a brake disc, 195 Note radial disc ve tilation chann

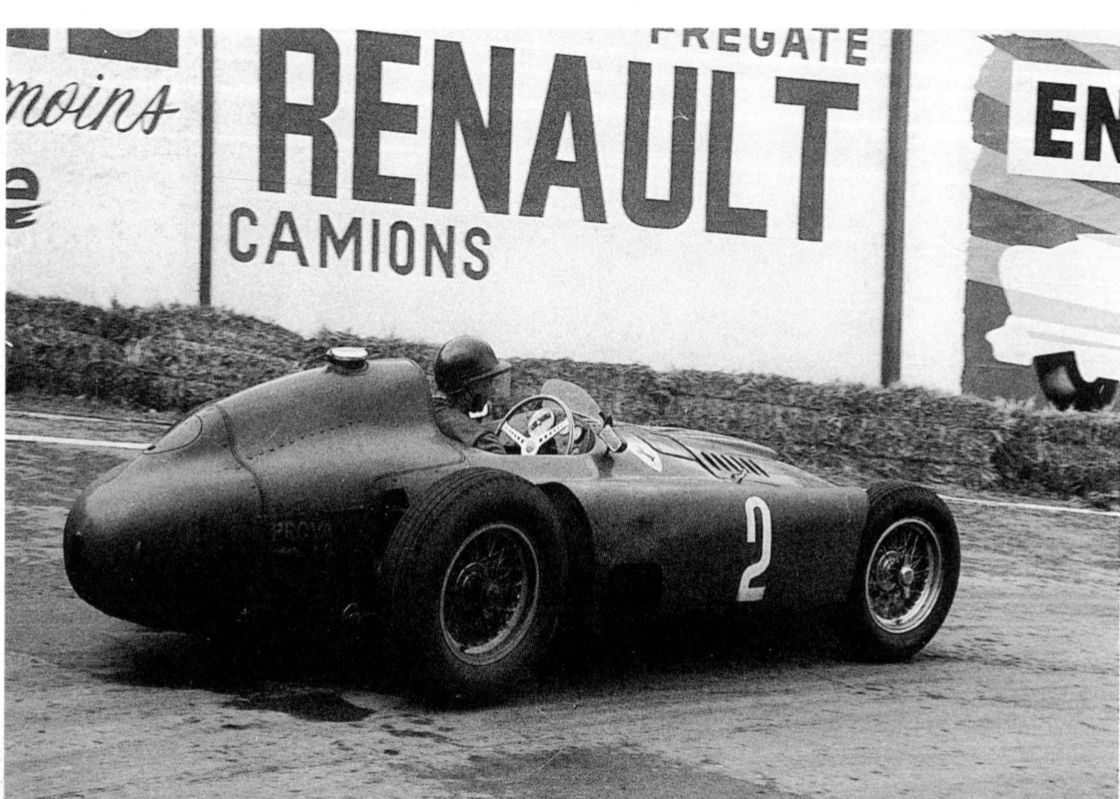

The oppositio This is reigni World Champi Fangio in the 19 Lancia-Ferrari Francorchamp

57

Bright Green

In the words of Motor Sport correspondent Denis Jenkinson: "At the end of the 1956 season a car was meticulously prepared for Stirling Moss to try, and after numerous long distance tests he agreed to sign up with Vandervell to lead the Vanwall team in the World Championship battle. To do this meant leaving the Maserati team, and they in turn signed on Fangio, the only driver who was superior to Moss. This now made the Vanwall future very bright, and it pleased Vandervell to think that the forthcoming season was not only going to be a battle between his green cars and the red ones, but that the two best drivers in the world were shared, one on each side".

With two years solid racing experience under its belt the hitherto undependable, somewhat erratic Vanwall had risen to the position of potential World Championship challenger. Meanwhile the rapid but jinxed BRM team had taken another blow with the departure of Brooks, who had frankly admitted to Mays that he had lost confidence in the car, as Hawthorn had earlier in the '56 season. For '57 Hawthorn remained at Ferrari alongside Collins and Castellotti while Brooks signed to join Moss at Vanwall. BRM was left with Flockhart and Salvadori.

Since leaving the BRM project, Vandervell had seen his private team steadily muster strength. Since taking BRM into private ownership, Owen had seen his team flatter only to deceive. With Moss at the wheel, the dark green Vanwall was now the formidable British challenger that the V16 BRM should have been. For his part, Moss was delighted as last to have a competitive British car backed by a sufficiently strong team. A team that could provide an adequate number of cars to ensure a full season's racing plus sufficient development and research to keep those cars in contention with the continental

The photographs the following eig pages show scen from Vanwall's fir Grand Prix winnir season. They illu trate, in order, Sa vadori at Roue (left), Mo following Behra Monte Carlo, Mo on his march victory at Pescar Brooks at Mon Carlo and Lewi Evans at Monz Note the shorten nose employed Monte Carl

20

BP
DUNLOP
EXTRA
ESSO
34

26

20

machinery.

Since Vanwall handling had left something to be desired in '56 Chapman had taken another look at the suspension and had prescribed coils in place of the rear leaf spring. Fichtel and Sachs dampers were also introduced, along with improved pot joints in the driveshafts to permit more rear wheel movement. Chapman had also added three degrees negative camber to the rear wheels, notwithstanding the de Dion system. His aim was to enhance grip at the rear, promoting more consistent understeer and Moss' satisfactory test at Oulton had been made with the coil springs. Moss had reported the handling much better than he had found at Silverstone for the International Trophy.

Otherwise the car was not significantly altered for 1957, aside from larger rear discs. Significantly though, Moss and Brooks were able to do a good deal of testing prior to the start of the '57 campaign, using a variety of UK circuits. An infuriating number of small, niggling problems arose and were tackled away from the pressure of racing.

Certainly Vandervell now had an armoury to match his equipment's potential: over the winter of '56/'57 he amassed enough equipment to ensure that no single car need be raced twice in succession. Still, for tax reasons, only four cars officially existed but there were two new frames and with that there were sufficient parts from which ten chassis could be assembled, though no more than seven 2.5 litre engines had been produced, following the two smaller displacement prototypes of '54. On the other hand, head production had reached 40 units.

The Park Royal team did not want for funding and only lack of a capable driver kept entries to two cars. However, once again Vandervell forsook the Argentine Grand Prix so as not to interfere with the development programme.

Kuzmicki had left the engine development programme to join the Humber company but remained a consultant for Vandervell, along with Craig and Weslake. Fuel development was continuing and Shell Mex & BP this year supplied the brew free of charge together with free castor-based oil and some financial support. Pirelli was winding -down its involvement in racing and needed some persuasion to continue to make tyres available.

Meanwhile Dunlop was looking for a liaison Vanwall but did not yet appear to have the measure of the Italian tyres. In February '57 comparative tests were carried out between Pirelli and Dunlop tyres, Dunlop offering a new nylon carcase version of its regular R3 racer. The normal cotton carcase wet weather R4 proved quickest in the wet while Pirelli was quickest in the dry. Vandervell retained Pirellis.

Jenkinson, who knew the man, reported that: "Vandervell could see his goal in sight when Moss signed to drive for him and... he threw everything into the battle, and worked and worried as much as anyone in the team. What had started out as a hobby, 'instead of playing golf' as he used to say, had turned into an obsession and he was now driving himself and the whole works at full pressure for he could see that the Italian teams were beginning to stumble in their efforts to stay ahead of his cars..."

DIARY

Park Royal (GB) January 13

As before the Vanwall team remained at home rather than contest the season opener at Buenos Aires which was thus a duel between Ferrari and Maserati once more. Moss had been released to drive for Maserati and he took pole but Fangio's sister new-style lightweight 250F won, the on-form Englishman delayed by a broken throttle.

Syracuse (I) April 7

Syracuse Grand Prix
Moss .... *Q: 3/R:3*
Brooks .... *Q: 4/R:NR*

Vanwall and Connaught - winner of this race in '55 and running four cars - had come down to Sicily to meet Maserati and Ferrari. Ferrari was running Collins and Musso who were quickest in practice, followed by the two Vanwalls, Behra and Schell, the latter pair heading the eight car Maserati challenge. Connaught could not match the pace.

Musso apparently made a jump start, Tony Brooks was also quick off the mark and the order at the end of the first lap was Musso, Brooks, Collins, Moss. Moss passed Collins on the second lap then on the third lap he swept into the lead and started drawing away. After six of 80 laps Brooks further demoted Musso who later fell back behind Collins. Collins then set about Brooks, passing him after 18 laps but all the while Moss was extending his lead.

Brooks felt an occasional misfire as a water leak affected his plugs. A joint on a brazed water pipe was failing but Brooks' pace was not unduly affected, Musso unable to better fourth. After 32 laps Moss came through with a rough sounding engine - a fuel line had broken. The next lap he came in for replacement at the cost of four laps. Just as that job was finished Brooks rolled to a halt, his engine well and truly cooked. Moss had rejoined seventh and by the end of the race, having consistently broken the lap record, he was third, three laps down on Collins and Musso.

Goodwood (GB) April 22

Glover Trophy
Moss .... *Q: 1/R:NR*
Brooks .... *Q: 2/R:6*

The Easter Monday Goodwood Formula One race pitted Vanwall against BRM and Connaught, BRM running Ron Flockhart and Salvadori. Connaught likewise ran two cars and three British club racers made up a nine car field. The Vanwalls were quickest in practice. Salvadori spun his BRM into retirement on the first lap and Flockhart spun down the order on the second. Thus, the two Vanwalls were left with a straightforward run home to victory over the Connaught team.

Alas, at the end of the sixth of 32 laps Brooks pitted with a broken throttle linkage which cost five laps to replace. Then at the end of the thirteenth lap Moss costed to a halt out on the circuit with the same problem. Stuart Lewis-Evans' Connaught won while Brooks finished last with a new lap record to document Vanwall's Goodwood pace.

Monte Carlo (MON) May 19

Monaco Grand Prix
Moss .... *Q: 3/R:NR*
Brooks .... *Q: 4/R:2*

The first European Grand Prix brought out works Maseratis for Fangio, Schell, Carlos Menditeguy and Giorgio Scarlatti and Ferraris for Collins, Hawthorn, Musso and Trintignant. Down from Britain were the Vanwalls for Moss and Brooks plus entries from BRM, Connaught and Cooper. Third on the grid, Moss was just three tenths slower than Collins' Ferra and was within a second of polema Fangio's lightweight 250F.

In the first day's practice Moss ha stolen the cash prize for fastest lap fro Fangio. Brooks lined up best of the re while the BRMs floundered. The BRM Salvadori failed to qualify, as did a se ond Cooper, the Cooper team starting 2.0 litre Climax mid-engine Formula Tw car for Jack Brabham from the back of th 16 car grid, along with the lone Co naught.

From the front row Moss jumped in an immediate lead chased by Fangi Collins, Schell, Brooks and Hawthor Collins soon moved up to second, the the two leaders broke away from th pack. However, on the fourth lap Mos brakes went away as a result of which h failed to negotiate the chicane. He left th track scattering poles and sandbags an the chaos claimed the Ferraris of Collir and Hawthorn as well as his own ca Thankfully Brooks was able to revers out of the melee, setting off still ahead Schell to chase Fangio who had uncar nily avoided the incident.

Brooks drove a plucky race but coul not dislodge Fangio, the Vanwall finish ing just 20 seconds in arrears after mo than three hours racing, running faul lessly throughout, its second place a ways secure.

Rouen (F) July 7

French Grand Prix
Salvadori .... *Q: 6/R:NR*
Lewis-Evans *Q:10/R:NR*

June was a bad month: the Belgian an Dutch Grands Prix succumbed to finar cial pressure, Brooks was injured at L Mans and Moss was taken ill. Thus, whe the Formula One circus resumed its shov at Rouen Vanwall was struggling onc more with two less established drivers. had taken Salvadori and Lewis-Evans o

Diary continues on page 60

Coming of Age

With Stirling Moss on board, Vanwall was ready to win Grand Prix races. At least, it was over the second half of the season, after Moss had suffered an uncharacteristic brake failure at Monaco, then had overcome his summer illness. May, June and early July 1957 was a wasted period for Moss (he also retired early in the Mille Miglia and early at Le Mans) but he subsequently won three of the remaining four World Championship races. That wasn't enough to dislodge Fangio's crown but it proved that the Vanwall had come of age.

During that memorable period between mid July and mid September Vanwall was finally a match for the Italian cars at circuits as diverse as Pescara and Monza - but not at the Nurburgring. In Germany the soft suspension afforded by the car's stiff frame worked against it, in spite of the bumpy nature of the track. On some parts of the circuit the Vanwalls had to back off while the harshly sprung Italian cars galloped flat out. With the Green Machine there was too much pitching and rolling and both Moss and Brooks finished the race physically sick.

The other flaw in the green challenge was a series of engine failures, which had started at Rouen and continued to take out one car each time at Aintree and Pescara. Subsequently, there was another engine failure at Casablanca.

aught driver s-Evans joined Vanwall team for ch Grand Prix ouen in view of enforced absence Moss and Brooks. worked his car o fifth before its er tank ex- ed under ure enough to the steering.

Diary continued

board, refugees from BRM and Connaught respectively.

Maserati had Fangio, Behra, Schell and Menditeguy, Ferrari had Collins, Hawthorn, Musso and Trintignant while Cooper and BRM again helped make up the numbers with two cars apiece, BRM with much modified chassis and MacKay Fraser alongside Flockhart. Maserati dominated practice and the best British car was Salvadori's Vanwall on the third row with Lewis-Evans representing the green on the fourth row.

Musso took the lead from Behra on the first lap, which the Vanwalls finished eighth (Salvadori) and twelfth. On the second lap Lewis-Evans moved up to ninth but Salvadori started losing oil from an unsecured filler cap, forcing a pit stop. Flockhart crashed on the oil. Meanwhile, teammate Fraser led Lewis-Evans, both cars out of the top six. The second BRM retired after 28 of 77 laps and at almost the same time Salvadori retired with two broken exhaust valve springs. Having inherited fifth, Lewis-Evans stopped around half distance with stiff steering and his engine overheating.

Fangio won again this weekend, with Musso second and Collins third.

Rheims (F) July 14

Rheims Grand Prix

Salvadori *Q:10/R:5*

Lewis-Evans ..... *Q: 2/R:3*

The circus moved East to Champagne country and the traditional home of the French Grand Prix for a non-championship race, the principal runners as at Rouen. However, Vanwall wheeled out a new streamlined car, which Lewis-Evans tried in the first practice. It was overgeared and its full potential remained unproven for its gearbox was commandeered overnight for one of the regular cars. In a regular car Lewis-Evans set a fastest lap bettered only by Fangio.

Maserati raced its new V12 car for the first time, in Menditeguy's hands. It incurred a one minute penalty for a push start and in any case was not quick enough to worry the serious runners. Lewis-Evans led on the first lap, chased by Fangio in a Monza offset 250F and Musso in an original, unmodified Lancia D.50. Then came Collins and Hawthorn in regular modified Lancia-Ferraris, followed by Salvadori.

Lewis-Evans pulled steadily away while Collins fell by the wayside and Hawthorn challenged Fangio as Musso led the pursuit of the flying Vanwall. Meanwhile, Salvadori slipped behind the regular 250Fs of Behra and Schell. On the 27th lap the flying Lewis-Evans lapped Salvadori while the retirement of Hawthorn left Fangio pressed by Behra. Musso then reeled in Lewis-Evans, the Vanwall suffering fading brakes and its driver finding his goggles obscured. On the 34th of 61 laps the Lancia went ahead.

Salvadori pitted for a few gallons of fuel, retaining sixth. On the 48th lap Fangio and Behra went ahead of Lewis-Evans, then Fangio spun off on oil. Thus Lewis-Evans finished third - with a front wheel locking - and Salvadori, two laps down on Musso, finished fifth.

Aintree (GB) July 20

British Grand Prix

Moss .... *Q: 1/R:NR*

Brooks .... *Q: 3/R:1 (Moss)*

Lewis-Evans.... *Q: 6/R:7*

Back on home soil and back to strength with the first Englishman ever to win the British Grand Prix heading the Vanwall challenge. Although Brooks was back as well, Vandervell retained the services of the impressive Lewis-Evans. Maserati fielded a quartet of straight eight cars for its regular drivers, Ferrari a similar number of runners, as usual. Again BRM a
Cooper factory cars made up the nu
bers - two apiece - while sadly the Co
naught factory had closed its doors.

Moss made a storming practice to a
nex pole, the first for Vanwall in Wor
Championship racing. Brooks was on
two tenths slower, sharing his time a
the front row with Behra's 250F. Lewi
Evans headed the third row, a seco
slower than Moss over the two minu
tour. Brooks still had a sore leg from h
Le Mans injuries so could not expect
sustain a high race pace.

Behra made the best start but Mo
overtook him on the first lap, the order
the end of the lap Moss, Behra, Brook
Hawthorn, Collins, Fangio. Moss stea
ily drew away while Fangio was passe
first by Musso then by Lewis-Evans. I
the eleventh of 90 laps Brooks had fall
back behind Hawthorn and Collins, th
Moss suffered a misfire and pitted to f
a loose plug lead, dropping back behi
Musso. Then he was in again to chan
plugs so after 26 laps Brooks was called
to hand over to him.

Moss rejoined ninth, over a minu
adrift of Behra's leading 250F. Broo
rejoined 16th in the sick car. By lap
Moss was closing in on Fangio's six
placed car and on lap 35 he demoted it.
couple of laps later Lewis-Evans mov
ahead of Collins for third, then Mo
moved ahead of Musso for fifth. Mo
was then 50 seconds behind Behra. C
lap 46 he passed Collins for fourth, th
set about Lewis-Evans, all the while r
ducing the deficit to Behra. In the proce
he became the first ever driver to l
Aintree at over 90m.p.h.

By lap 62 Moss was third and only
seconds from Behra, by lap 68, only 28
seconds. Then suddenly the two Vanwa
came around in the lead. Behra's engi
had failed and Hawthorn had picked
a puncture, possibly from fragments
Maserati straight six. Alas, after thr

Diary continues on page 62

·ks at Monte lo, chasing a Con- ght down to the abeau corner. owing the early lent that elimi- d Moss and the kest Ferraris, ks held second to gio and there he ed for the ainder of the race.

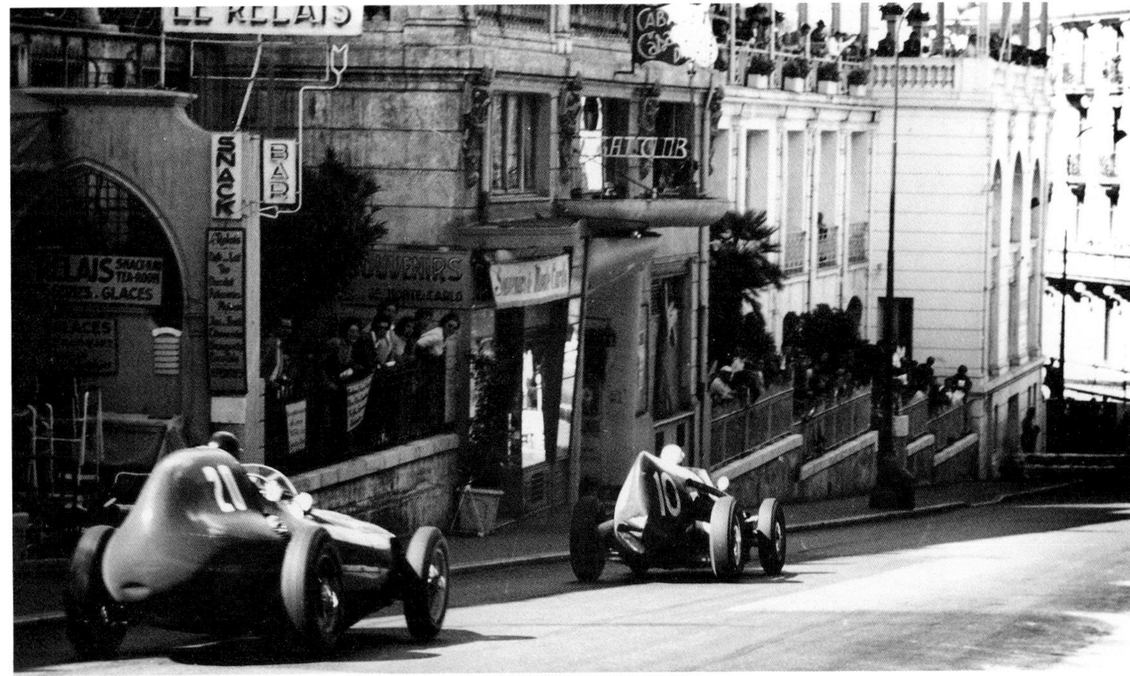

However, it is possible that Salvadori's Rouen failure was down to the driver over-revving the engine during the spin he undertook on his own oil.

Hairpin springs from Germany as seen in '56 had not been the answer to on going valve spring failures: Vandervell simply had to painstakingly test each and every spring on a rig to weed out the poor ones. Both Mahle and Hepworth pistons were evaluated, Hepworth introducing an improved alloy, 'RR59'. Piston ring blow-bye led to oil mist billowing from Lewis-Evans' breather at Rheims: this was the root of his fading brakes, and it also blackened his goggles and gloves.

At Aintree a spare car was equipped with an experimental head which thanks to revised porting had higher power over the 3500-5000r.p.m. band with the same top end. It was in this region that the standard engine had a bad flat spot. Moss later recalled: "overcoming that flat spot was one of the major problems, equalled only by the difficulty in convincing the Chief it was there". This season power was quoted as 285b.h.p. at 7300r.p.m. on a compression ratio of 12.5:1 with at least 10b.h.p more available through the use of nitromethane (thus a figure of over 16b.h.p. per litre per 1000r.p.m. was attainable).

Indeed, 1957 was the year of nitromethane, as evidenced by tears in the eyes of pit staff. As we have seen, in previous years the usual brew had been a blend of methanol and benzole, the latter rating only 100 octane but helping keep consumption in check. Methanol, like all alcohol fuels carries its own oxygen, enabling a richer mixture to be exploited. The next step is nitromethane, which carries more of its own oxygen but is destructive in its effect on engine internals.

A typical highly potent '57 blend was 80% methanol, 15% acetone and 5% eye-watering nitromethane. In general, it was reckoned that methanol was worth a 10% power boost over benzole while nitromethane gave an additional power boost of around half the percentage added. Thus, a hypothetical engine capable of producing 250b.h.p. on 100 octane fuel would give 275b.h.p. on pure methanol and an extra 2.5% power with 5% of its fuel nitromethane, taking its output to 280.5b.h.p. That was the sort of figure quoted this season.

Ferrari frequently resorted to nitro, particularly in qualifying. For the Vanwall engine Weslake recommended a blend of 27% benzole, 27% Avgas, 36% methanol or ethanol and 10% nitromethane. Ethanol was preferred over

Diary continued

more laps Lewis-Evans struck throttle linkage trouble, the adventure dropping him to seventh at the finish, eight laps down. But thankfully Moss was not denied his triumph, the triumph he had so much wanted: winning in a British car on home soil, with a new lap record as well.

Nurburgring (D) August 4

German Grand Prix
Moss .... Q: 7/R:5
Brooks .... Q: 5/R:9
Lewis-Evans ..... Q: 9/R:NR

Four from Maserati, three from Ferrari and three from Vanwall comprised the line up of works Formula One cars at the 'Ring, BRM withdrawing from the race. Vanwall arrived early and found its handling wanting over the sinuous, undulating mountain course, the cars pitching around in places, making life very uncomfortable for the drivers. In contrast, the stiffer sprung red cars were closely matched, Fangio taking pole by less than three seconds from Hawthorn. Brooks was 10.5 second slower than Fangio, though that represented only a 2% deficit: a fine effort on a Bucking Bronco.

The race saw Hawthorn, Collins, Fangio, Behra, Musso and Schell slot into the top positions ahead of Brooks, Moss and Lewis-Evans. Moss overtook Brooks on the second lap, then Lewis-Evans followed him through. Lewis-Evans then overtook Moss only to suffer transmission seizure, spinning out at Kesselchen. Still the remaining Vanwalls could make no impression on the Italian cars.

However, the Maseratis had started on half tanks and after refuelling Behra and Schell finished behind Moss, who ran home a lonely fifth and on the verge of collapse. Musso was a lonely fourth but there was plenty of excitement at the front as Fangio recovered from his refuelling stop to beat Hawthorn and Collins with an epic drive. Brooks found the choppy ride too much and came home a lap down having been physically sick.

Pescara (I) August 18

Pescara Grand Prix
Moss .... Q: 2/R:1
Brooks .... Q: 6/R:NR
Lewis-Evans ..... Q: 8/R:5

Pescara was a new World Championship event this year. It presented 16 miles of everyday roads and Ferrari boycotted the event, having a policy against racing on Italian public highway. However, the factory lent a car to Musso since he retained an outside chance of beating Fangio to the World Championship crown. Maserati presented its 'Ring line up while the British Racing Green was carried by a pair of Formula Two Climax-Coopers as well as the Vanwall trio. Maserati 250F privateers comprised the balance of the 16 car field.

Though Fangio took pole, Moss was in cracking form, overtaking early leader Musso on the second of 18 laps. Behra and Fangio were next up while Brooks had retired from fifth with a blown piston after only one lap. That left Lewis-Evans fifth but he soon lost a tread and the same thing happened the next time around with a fresh tyre.

Nevertheless, Moss was firmly in command and he led all the way home, in spite of a stop after 12 of 18 laps to check fluctuating oil pressure. More oil was added and a loose filler cap was tightened. Moss' fastest lap, set on lap nine, had equalled Fangio's pole time. Fangio had to settle for second after Musso retired but that ensured he retained the World Championship crown. Lewis-Evans came home in fifth place, a lap down and grappling with a sticking throttle.

Monza (I) September 8

Italian Grand Prix
Moss .... Q: 2/R:1
Brooks .... Q: 3/R:7
Lewis-Evans ..... Q: 1/R:NR

The banking was not in use this yea Vanwall's strong combination of engi power and aerodynamic efficiency pa dividends on Monza's fast road circu the organisers had to expand the fro row of the grid to four cars to have splash of red on it. Surprisingly, Lewi Evans headed the trio of green machine his time half a second under Brooks' thi fastest clocking. Fangio was another tw tenths slower in the first of the Italian ca after trading fastest lap with Moss in th first day's practice for which there was 200,000 lire prize. The Vanwall driv had claimed it.

Behra headed the second row drivin the still unfamiliar, still undependab and thirsty V12 Maserati: racing it was desperate measure in the face of Vanwall pace. Schell and Scarlatti handled regul 250Fs to complete the Modena quart while Maranello likewise was runnin four cars. The rest of the grid comprise private (or quasi-factory) 250Fs.

Moss shot into the lead with Muss forging ahead of the other Vanwalls, the Behra ahead of Fangio. Behra then move up to second as Musso slipped back t fifth and Collins overtook Fangio. Fang speeded up after the first few laps an Schell's Maserati likewise came into th picture. After five of 87 laps, six car made the front running in a slipstream ing bunch: the three Park Royal warrior Behra, Fangio and Schell.

Behra and Moss traded the lead, the Fangio led, then Brooks and Lewis-Evan both took turns in front. The Vanwall were able to play with the Maseratis bu after 20 laps Brooks had to pit for a stick ing throttle. Three laps later Lewis-Evan also pitted, with stiff steering. Moss le firmly after 25 laps and soon Behra stoppe

Diary continues on page 64

methanol for its higher calorific value, which reduced consumption. However, piston life was very marginal with nitromethane. A nitromethane engine - with sodium cooled inlet as well as exhaust valves - was run in the non-championship race at Morocco, but only in the spare car. It gave an extra 9 - 10b.h.p. all the way from 6,000 - 7,000r.p.m. A nitro test engine gave a flash reading of 308b.h.p. on the bench.

In total, in 1957 Vanwall made 16 World Championship starts and brought its cars home on nine occasions, its three wins backed up by one second and five lowly finishes. Of the seven retirements, one was the aforementioned Monaco incident, three were the aforementioned engine failures. That leaves just one gearbox failure, one steering failure that arose through engine failure and one throttle/pump linkage failure. The overall level of reliability was reasonable if not exceptional. Better might have been expected given the constant deployment of fresh equipment.

Still the vibration of the four cylinder engine was cause for concern, as witness the pump linkage failure. At Syracuse vibration led to an injector pipe fracture reminiscent of earlier seasons which cost Moss the race, and vibration split a water pipe on the other car. At Goodwood the throttle/pump linkage broke on both cars, this again an old familiar vibration-related failure. For the Monaco Grand Prix the metal injector feed lines were replaced by flexible rubber tubing to aircraft standards and a short length of the new tubing was used as a joint in the control linkage which was subject both to vibration and a torsional loading. This tubing was so called 'Silvoflex' supplied by the Palmer Tyre Company.

The introduction of Silvoflex stopped the injector line failures but still the control linkage played up at Aintree and Monza. In retrospect it would have been better not to have rigidly mounted the pump on the front of the engine. Another inherent problem was the proximity ofthe header tank to the steering linkage. It was possible for an over-pressurised header tank to

wis-Evans chases awthorn's Ferrari ır 14) and Fraser's RM (car 28) at uen. This was, wever, a Maserati ce, Fangio's 250F nning. Overleaf, oss is pictured at scara where he ok the lead on the cond lap and ran way to victory, anwall's second ccess of the season, llowing the Aintree ost.

Diary continued

at the pits leaving only Fangio, Schell and Collins on the lead lap. Brooks had a recurrence of his throttle problem and fell right out of the reckoning.

Moss was meanwhile steadily drawing away from Fangio and by lap 31 Fangio was the only other runner on the same lap. Fangio had started on half tanks and had to refuel and after this Moss was able to put the World Champion a lap down. At the other end of the field, Lewis-Evans retired his delayed car with overheating after 57 laps. Moss later made a precautionary stop, such was his lead and he then finished with 40 seconds over Fangio, the only other runner on the lead lap. Meanwhile Brooks had set fastest lap regaining ground and he finished seventh, five laps down.

Goodwood (GB) September 28

Tony Vandervell agreed that Moss could make a ten lap demonstration run at Goodwood in his Monza winning car. However, this decision he came to regret since the engine expired before the exercise was over...

Casablanca (MOR) October 27

Moroccan Grand Prix
Moss .... Withdrew
Brooks........... Q: 1/R:NR
Lewis-Evans ..... Q: 3/R:2

Although three Vanwalls were entered for the non-championship Moroccan Grand Prix on the new Casablanca circuit, Moss was struck down by Asian 'flu after setting fastest time on the first day. Others affected were Fangio and Hawthorn, though both were able to race. Maserati ran four regular 250Fs, Ferrari two Avgas burning Dino V6 models, Collins driving a 2.4 litre version, Hawthorn a 2.2 litre example. BRM ran two cars, as did Cooper.

Brooks took pole from Behra's 250F and Lewis-Evans but Behra made the best start. However, Collins exploited the light fuel load of his conservatively fuelled Ferrari to pass Behra on the first lap, coming around with a healthy advantage. Next up were Behra, Lewis-Evans and Brooks. Collins spun his advantage away on the second lap, continuing in second place while Brooks moved ahead of Lewis-Evans. After 11 laps Brooks overtook Collins only to retire with magneto failure. Collins then crashed out, leaving Lewis-Evans second until Fangio overtook, the Vanwall suffering a stiff gear change. However, Fangio then spun.

With his sticking gear change Lewis-Evans could not catch Behra and near the end the Vanwall ran low on fuel, spluttering home. Had he not slowed with the gear problem he would have needed more fuel. Trintignant's BRM bagged third as Fangio found further problems.

swell sufficiently to jam the steering. This was Lewis-Evan's problem at Rouen (water loss from a head crack pressurising the tank) and on other occasions drivers found stiffened steering. A sticking throttle was another occasional headache: at Pescara it delayed Lewis-Evans, at Monza, Brooks.

Aside from the 'Ring it was clear that the Vanwall was now a strong all round contender. Moss was within a second of Fangio's pole time at Monaco and was within ten seconds at Pescara over a lap of 15.9 rather than 1.9 miles. While the average speed at Monte Carlo was under 70m.p.h. Pescara was a swings and roundabouts affair with a slow average in the mountains offset by a couple of fast legs that lifted the overall average speed close to 100m.p.h. - faster than Aintree (around 90m.p.h.) if a lot slower than Monza (almost 125m.p.h. in spite of the lack of banking).

At Pescara Lewis-Evans was timed fastest at 182m.p.h. Further, at Monza, and at the non-championship Rheims race in Lewis-Evans' inexperienced hands the Vanwall confirmed its reputation for high speed circuit performance. Fast circuit lap times showed the worth of Costin's aerodynamic concept while the general deportment of the car indicated that Chapman's chassis work had come right. However, the car was heavy to handle and had to be driven more precisely than the Maserati 250F with which this season Fangio perfected the technique of four wheel drift.

The 250F was a 'chuckable' car with a tendency towards oversteer: the Vanwall had a tendency towards understeer and had to be driven more precisely. The Vanwall also suffered a heavy, somewhat difficult gearchange. At Monte Carlo Brooks lost his clutch early on and after finishing second to Fangio his left hand looked "like a plate of meat", in his own words.

Again, there was no significant chassis development during the course of the season. At Rouen VW8 was introduced with lighter tubing for the frame, 20s.w.g. rather than 18s.w.g. The most notable modification was a shortened nose and cut down screen for Monaco, where drag was of relatively low importance. The truncated nose was fitted with a bracing bar across the radiator and helped avoid damage in the crowded opening laps, also assisting cooling in the Mediterranean heat. The cut down screen improved visibility and cockpit ventilation. There was also additional steering lock for Monte Carlo while the engine was tuned - via camshaft profiling - for additional low speed torque at the expense of around 10b.h.p. worth top end power.

At the other end of the speed spectrum was Rheims, for which Vanwall prepared an enclosed wheel special. In fact, Costin faired in only the front wheels, feeling that to have enclosed the rear wheels as well would not have been worth the implicit weight penalty. It took him a month or so to draw the revised shape, which was produced via new panels grafted onto the existing outline of VW6. Alas, its performance was not put to the test...

Meanwhile, BRM fortunes sank to an ever lower ebb, notwithstanding assistance from Chapman, here again working as a consultant. Following Chapman's advice BRM radically modified its chassis but it did not have a worthy driver aside from Behra who drove the car in the non-championship Caen Grand Prix and Silverstone International Trophy events, winning both.

In World Championship racing all Vanwall's serious opposition came from south of the Alps. It was a three cornered fight between Park Royal, Modena and Maranello with the best drivers well distributed between the three camps, hence the problem facing BRM.Of course, Vandervell had set out running only two cars since

he didn't have access to a third driver capable of doing justice to the team. He found that man in Lewis-Evans, who wound up on pole at Monza. Overall, still Fangio and Moss were the two Aces, which put Maserati in a stronger position than Ferrari.

If the latest lightweight version of the 250F was good enough to take Fangio to another World Championship, in no way was it an exceptional car. It was, however, spot on from the word go and its strength was in its all round ability. It was competitive on circuits as diverse as Monaco and Monza while Fangio was now in his prime. However, only at Buenos Aires - the race from which Vanwall was absent - and Rouen (which Moss missed through illness) did

Start of the Italian Grand Prix Monza: three Brit cars heading the fr row, Lewis-Evans pole, Brooks mak the sharpest getaw

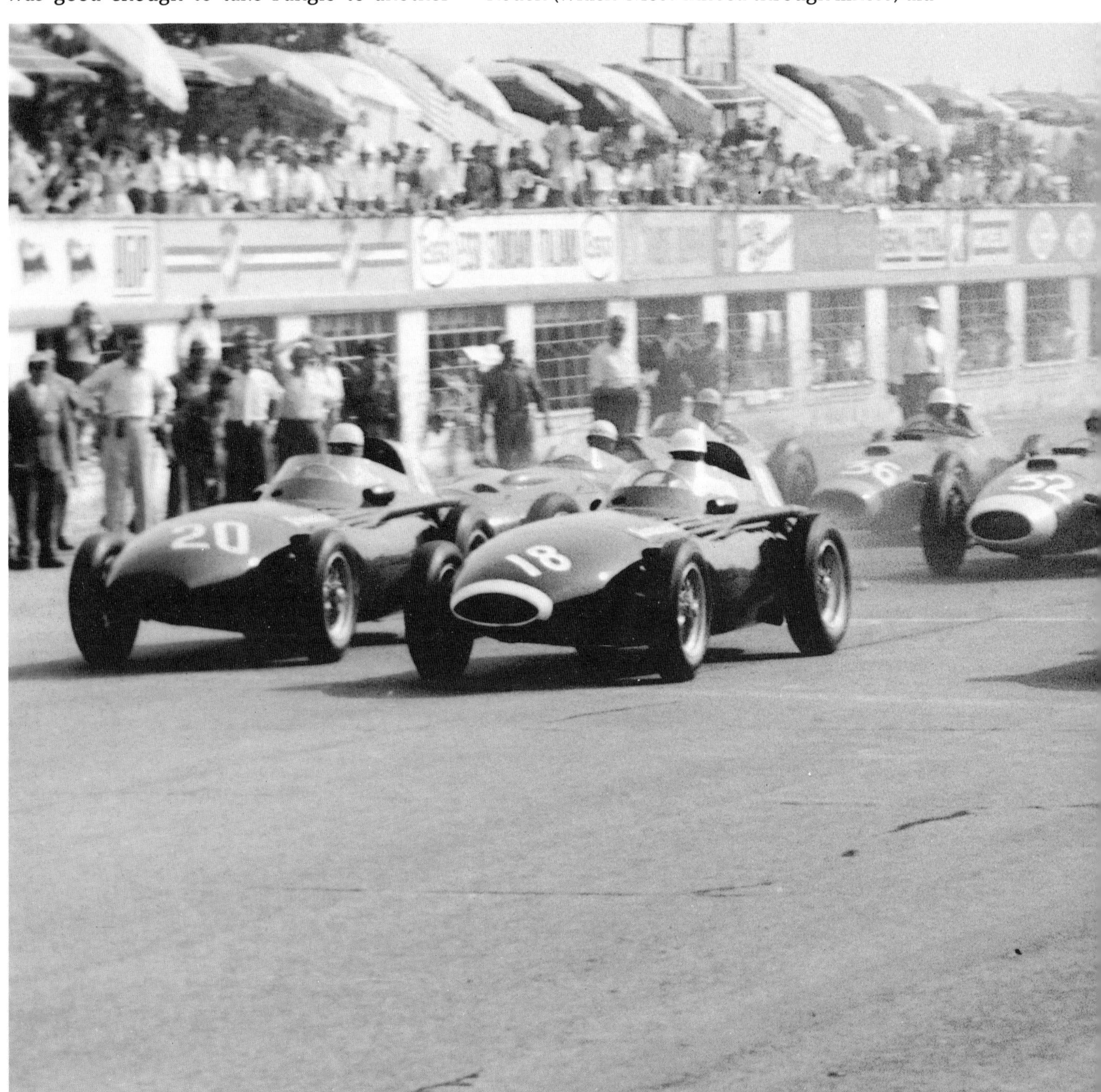

the previous ad, Brooks is seen ing Moss and is-Evans at the burgring. The wall was less petitive in Ger- ny.

Fangio dominate in the style of old. Meanwhile, Ferrari was often a threat but only really came into focus at the Nurburgring.

The further modified D.50 was a disappointment, a useful points gatherer but not a natural race winner in the hands of Hawthorn, Collins and Musso. The car had a bigger bore engine but that did not appear to unleash stronger horses while the chassis modifications - which included discarding the distinctive panniers altogether - lacked direction. Coil springs were introduced for the front suspension, and for an experimental swing axle rear suspension that echoed Daimler-Benz' successful layout of '54/'55. That might have been forward thinking but there was also a regressive semi-

ladder frame as all trace of Jano's adventurous 1954 concept faded.

Faced with an uncharacteristic lack of power, Ferrari put all effort into an all new Jano V6 petrol engine for 1958. Meanwhile, Maserati toyed with a V12 engine, another important project with a view to forthcoming fuel restrictions. However, this season the twelve cylinder engine was far from driveable with all its power at the top end and consequently was not a factor, except at Monza.

Of the three key engines, the Maserati six and Ferrari V8 ran similar speeds, the 250F now capable of sustaining 8,700r.p.m. without coming apart. However, running 1000r.p.m. more than the Vanwall four was not a distinct advantage, thanks mainly to the continuing development of exotic fuel. With a Witches' Brew in the tank there was little place for mechanical sophistication: all three well developed engines were capable of an output in the region of 280 - 300b.h.p. given the right chemical mix. With fuel restricted to commercial blends for the following season, the British four cylinder exponents had genuine tears in their eyes as the curtain came down on a memorable year...

Monza: Fangi lightweight 25 mixes it with Vanwall trio. Lew Evans and Bro met trouble but M beat the Wo Champion's Maser by almost a lap

58

Gas Burner

Vanwall motored into 1958 in top gear, its strength the equal of any. Indeed, World Champion Fangio was threatening retirement as Maserati closed its competition department. The four cylinder BRM had still not lived up to its early promise and 1958 was shaping up as Vanwall versus Ferrari, with a familiar trio of British drivers in the British cars and compatriots Hawthorn and Collins leading the red attack, along with Musso who was representing the hopes of the Italian population. Park Royal's drivers formed a well knit band and the London team wanted for nothing. Vandervell knew this year his outfit was ripe for World Championship success and - as ever - ensured that it had all the means at its disposal.

The only real uncertainty over the new season was the effect of the switch to Avgas fuel, since the existing engines had been developed to thrive on a highly potent brew, this, as we have seen, providing a beneficial internal cooling effect and allowing a very high compression ratio. For Vanwall, exotic fuel had helped mask the relative lack of sophistication of a simple four cylinder power plant.

Henceforth, less fuel would need to be carried since the mandatory Avgas boasted a higher calorific value and in addition, race distances were reduced, from three to two hours, this also allowing cars to run without a tyre stop. The overall effect was to encourage a trend towards smaller, lighter Formula Two style cars, giving the funny little mid engined Climax-Cooper a better chance.

Vandervell considered lightening via the use of titanium but the material did not prove compatible with the needs of the chassis components for which it might have been employed, such as the de Dion tube and the discs. However, a new style of "wobbly web" aluminium alloy wheel proved beneficially lighter than the traditional wire spoke wheel, making an important saving in unsprung weight.

Vanwall now looked to Dunlop for its rubber, Pirelli having withdrawn. The team carefully prepared its ten existing chassis for the new season, again assembling no more than four at a time for tax reasons. Aside from engine modifications appropriate to the change of fuel there were few changes. The tail was slightly reshaped, the exhaust tail pipe became less protrusive and there were suspension modifications - most notably a thinner front anti roll bar, reducing understeer - appropriate to the new conditions and in particular to the new tyres from Fort Dunlop in Birmingham.

The photographs the next eight pag depict scenes fro the Vanwall's Wor Manufacturer Championsh winning season. order, they portr Brooks at Rhei (left) chasing a Fe rari, Lewis-Evans Spa Fra corchamps, Lew Evans at Cas blanca, Brooks Spa Francorcham (en route to victo and Lewis-Evans Rheims. The no damage evident Lewis-Evans' car Francorchamps w caused by an ear collision wi Gendebien's Ferra

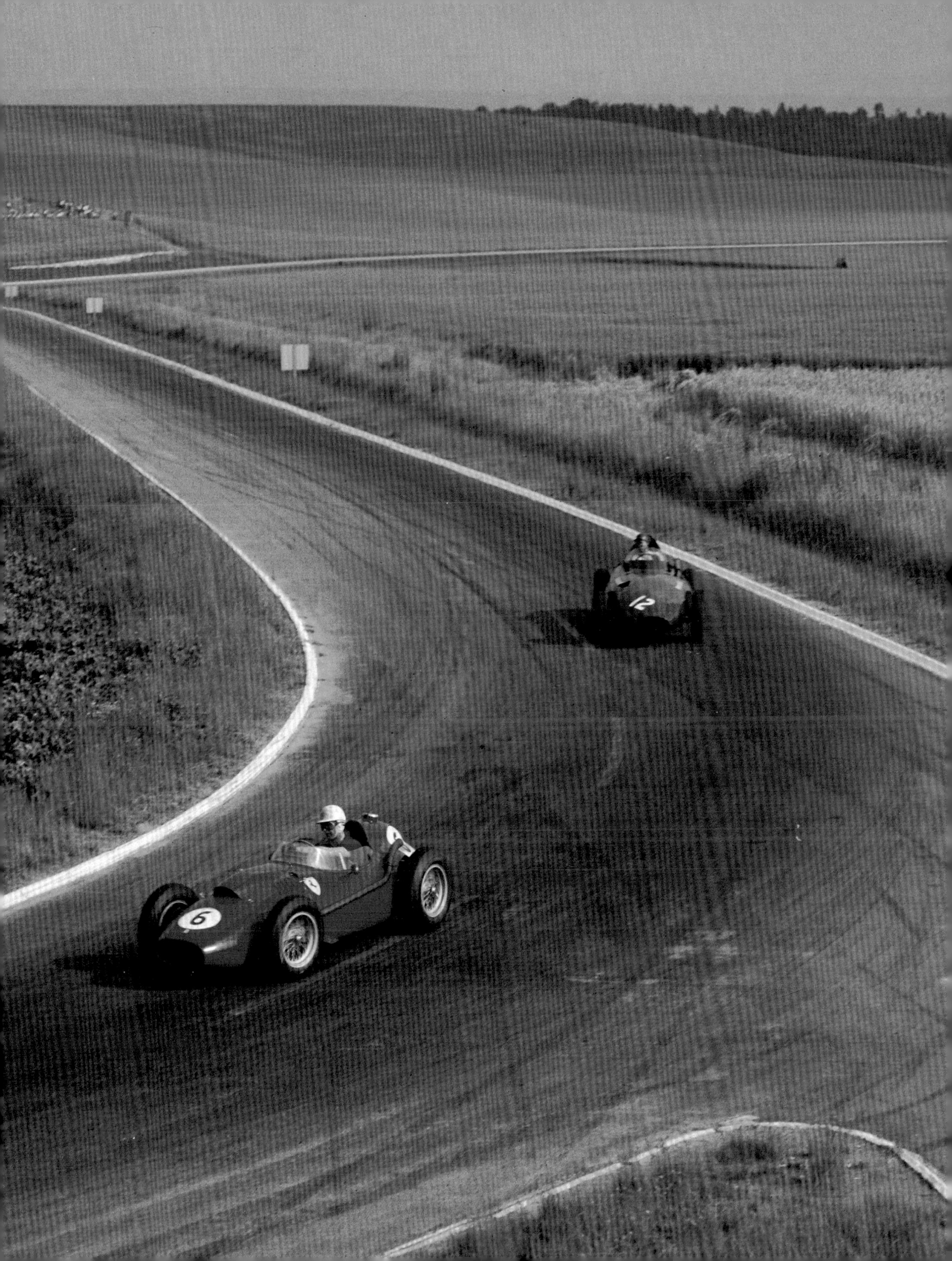

12

4

12
Vanwall

A Safe Bet ?

Vanwall entered the 1958 season on the crest of a wave, the only cloud on the horizon the disadvantage of running a highly stressed four cylinder engine on the mandatory Avgas. However, the sophisticated V12 Maserati had come to nought - the once feared marque and its World Champion slipping into virtual retirement - while Ferrari had switched from a V8 to a relatively simple V6 engine. Fangio's withdrawal had left Moss the King of Grand Prix racing and it remained merely to crown him: a safe bet, or so it must have seemed to the gamblers enjoying the world's most famous casino at the start of the European season.

Why, the Golden Boy had already won the Argentine Grand Prix at the wheel of Rob Walker's funny little mid engine Cooper. With formidable support from Brooks and Lewis-Evans all looked set for a memorable year of Park Royal Green. At Zandvoort, Francorchamps, the Nurburgring, Oporto, Monza and Casablanca the London team did indeed triumph, but on three occasions Brooks was at the wheel, Team Leader Moss by the wayside. That mattered not all in the chase for the Manufacturer's Cup, which Vandervell won in convincing fashion, but it did mean that Moss gathered less World Championship points than was his due.

Brooks and Lewis-Evans gave Moss tremendous support, as expected, and the Manufacturers' Cup was deservedly won. But the new Cup was not something that the public at large understood, not what the gamblers had staked money on. Everyone understood that Moss was looking for the World title that he so richly deserved at the wheel of a Vanwall. At Monaco he retired. At Francorchamps he retired, having missed a gear and buzzed the engine. At Rheims he had to give second best to Hawthorn's Ferrari. At the Nurburgring he retired. At Monza he retired. Aside from Rheims, when Moss finished he finished in first place. A locking front brake cost him victory at Rheims. The World Championship title went to fellow countryman Hawthorn by the margin of one point.

A year, then, of mixed feelings and of mixed fortunes for England's hero. But one of success for the car, and that arguably counted above all. After all, Vandervell's mission was always to put the Green to the fore, and that he most certainly did in '58. Fangio used to say: "when I drive, I drive for the team and for the car..." On that basis Moss' year was a success but frustration at having missed the title was justified.

World Champion Hawthorn had signalled his intent by leading early on in Argentina then setting fastest lap alongside the Mediterranean. The V6 Ferrari had a very impressive engine, if a mediocre chassis. At Zandvoort the Ferrari team was off form but at Francorchamps both pole position and fastest lap went the way of Hawthorn. Again he took fastest lap at Rheims, and of course he won. It was his first and only win of the season, though Ferrari did not lose form.

Collins won Silverstone with Hawthorn second and another fastest lap to Hawthorn's credit. At the 'Ring the 'Farnham Flyer' took his third pole position of four races while at Oporto he took another fastest lap. Both in Germany and in Portugal Ferrari's retention of drum brakes cost it dear. At the 'Ring the Ferrari power advantage might well have been its winning edge, had Brooks not had the advantage of superior handling and superior, fade-free braking. Brake failure appears to have contributed to Collins' crash.

Tragically, the season that put British cars to the fore (together Vanwall and Cooper won seven of the nine races) and which was dominated by British drivers (Trintignant at Monaco

DIARY

Park Royal (GB) January 19

As usual Vandervell declined to send his cars to Argentina - delays by the organising club were blamed - and on this occasion Moss hitched a ride in Rob Walker's 2.0 litre mid engine Climax-Cooper. With the works Maserati team disbanded Fangio drove a loaned 250F, which he put on pole ahead of the Dino V6 Ferraris of Hawthorn, Collins and Musso and the 250F of Behra. Suffering a bandaged eye, Moss was down in mid grid but he was fit on race day and the light, agile and frugal Cooper took him through to significant victory on the hot, twisty circuit.

Monte Carlo (MON) May 18
Monaco Grand Prix
Moss .... *Q: 8/R:NR*
Brooks .... *Q: 1/R:NR*
Lewis-Evans ..... *Q: 7/R:NR*

The Grand Prix world re-assembled on the Riviera with Vanwall present but Fangio absent, the World Champion having hung his helmet. Trintignant took over the Walker Cooper while Brabham and Salvadori drove a similar works cars, these nimble machines going well on the tight town circuit. Indeed, using a 2.2 litre engine Brabham made the front row, beaten only by Brooks and Behra's BRM while Salvadori and Trintignant were next up, using 2.0 litre engines. Moss was suffering a stomach complaint, hence his midfield start.

A second slower than Brooks, Behra was backed by Schell while other works entries came from Ferrari - Hawthorn, Collins, Musso and Wolfgang von Trips in the latest Dino V6 cars - and Lotus with two examples of its new Climax powered car which was front engined but notably small. Hawthorn was sixth fastest, with Lewis-Evans and Moss completing the top half of the 16 car grid. With only two of nine privately entered 250Fs qualifying, ten of the 16 runners were in British cars.

Behra took the lead at the start, from Brooks, Brabham, Moss, Trintignant and Lewis-Evans. The first red car was Hawthorn's Ferrari in seventh place but he steadily worked up to third at eight (of 100) laps, ahead of Moss who had demoted Brabham. Meanwhile, Lewis-Evans dropped back, soon to retire with steering trouble possibly the result of an incident at the first corner. Hawthorn's drive took him ever closer to Brooks who was losing power and after 18 laps the Ferrari came through second. Three laps later Brooks abandoned his car with a sick engine, a plug have fallen out.

After 27 laps Hawthorn's rousing drive took him ahead of Behra, then the BRM found trouble, elevating Moss to second. Moss then closed in on Hawthorn and he took the lead on lap 32 but could not shake the Ferrari off his tail. At the end of 38 laps Hawthorn came through in the lead once more and Moss stopped at his pit. A tappet had broken. The race was seemingly left to Ferrari but Hawthorn's car broke and teammates Musso and Collins could not dislodge Trintignant's Walker Cooper.

Zandvoort (NL) May 25
Dutch Grand Prix
Moss .... *Q: 2/R:1*
Brooks .... *Q: 3/R:NR*
Lewis-Evans ..... *Q: 1/R:NR*

Through the sweeps between the dunes there was nothing to touch Vanwall speed: the front row was Park Royal Green, with Behra's BRM and Brabham's 2.2 litre Climax-Cooper keeping the red cars down to the third row. The key players were as at Monte Carlo and the on-form Lewis-Evans was nine tenths of a second faster than Moss, a full second faster than Brooks in practice. Hawthorn's quickest Ferr[a]ri was another second adrift. Lacking pa[ce] no more competitive than the 2.0 lit[re] Climax cars, Ferrari was running thr[ee] cars, having dropped von Trips.

Moss made the best start, followed [by] Lewis-Evans and Schell, Brooks next [,] ahead of Brabham. After only three la[ps] Brooks came in to check the rear end [of] his car and he retired after a dozen la[ps] with rear axle failure. Meanwhile, Sch[ell] had overtaken Lewis-Evans but cou[ld] not stop Moss drawing away. On t[he] 32nd of 75 laps Moss achieved his targ[et] of a new lap record, at this stage holdi[ng] almost half a second over Schell. T[he] situation at the front then remained sta[ble] but after 46 laps Lewis-Evans retired wi[th] valve trouble, leaving the BRMs seco[nd] and third. They were the only other ca[rs] to finish on the lead lap.

Spa Francorchamps (B) June 15
Belgian Grand Prix
Moss .... *Q: 3/R:NR*
Brooks .... *Q: 5/R:1*
Lewis-Evans *Q:11/R:3*

After its poor showing in Holland, Fe[r]rari found renewed speed on the fast sweeps between the Ardennes' pine cl[ad] hills. Hawthorn and Musso both out-ra[n] Moss in practice, while Collins and Gend[e]bien (replacing von Trips) sandwich[ed] Brooks. Only these six drivers broke t[he] four minute barrier. BRM and Coop[er] were less competitive on this circuit. Coop[er] had lost the support of Walker's third c[ar] and had a 2.2 litre car for Salvadori and 2.0 litre for Brabham, while likewise L[o]tus had one 2.2 litre, one 2.0 litre Clima[x].

Moss snatched the lead at the start, fo[l]lowed by Brooks, Gendebien and Behr[a]. Alas, Moss missed a gear on the first l[ap] and buzzed the engine, ending his da[y]. Thus, Brooks led at the completion of t[he] first lap with Collins up to second ahe[ad] of teammates Gendebien and Hawtho[rn]

Diary continues on page 84

nte Carlo 1958: oks (30) and Moss lead Trintig- t's Climax-Cooper ugh the station pin. All three walls retired this opening of the European on and the little Walker entered engine car came ugh to win.

the only outsider) claimed the lives of two of the country's finest, Collins and Lewis-Evans. Earlier, at Rheims, Musso had crashed fatally. For Vandervell, the loss of Lewis-Evans at the wheel of one of his creations took away much of the joy of beating the red cars fairly and squarely.

To cap it all, just three months into his reign Hawthorn was killed in a road accident. With Vanwall pulling out of competition, it was clear that the face of Grand Prix racing had changed almost out of recognition in the course of one remarkable year of British Triumph and British Tragedy.

Indeed, far sighted observers saw the future in that compact, agile Cooper which went so well at Monaco and at Silverstone. The Cooper had the wind of change on its side: lighter fuel loads and shorter race distances were in favour of the funny little device with its low frontal area, low centre of gravity and ease of handling. Consider that the double Grand Prix winning 'Fairground Special' had less than 200b.h.p. at its disposal in '58.

The fuel switch had, of course, cut power, the mandatory Avgas slashing power for Vanwall from around 285b.h.p. to less than 270b.h.p.

Diary continued

with Behra fifth and Lewis-Evans sixth. On the next lap Collins took Hawthorn and Musso took Lewis-Evans but on the third lap Brooks still had the advantage while Behra dropped back, elevating the second Vanwall back to sixth position.

Thus, the race was Vanwall versus Ferrari and Collins led at the end of the fourth lap. Then Gendebien had a slight off, Collins' engine failed and Musso crashed, all of which promoted Lewis-Evans to third. Hawthorn could not catch Brooks and Lewis-Evans could not catch Hawthorn while fourth was the best of the 'rabbits': Cliff Allison's 2.2 litre Climax-Lotus. After 10 of 24 laps Brooks had a thirty second advantage and the race ran out as stalemate, the main interest the battle for fourth between the Climax cars which eventually went to Allison.

Brooks' Vanwall won in spite of its gearbox jamming on the last lap while Hawthorn took second (with fastest lap to his credit) in spite of his engine blowing in sight of the flag and Lewis-Evans collected third in spite of his rear suspension collapsing almost on the line!

Rheims (F) July 6
French Grand Prix
Moss .... *Q: 6/R:2*
Brooks .... *Q: 5/R:NR*
Lewis-Evans ..... *Q:10/R:NR (Brooks)*

Hawthorn backed up pole and fastest lap at Francorchamps with fastest lap at Rheims, over one and a half seconds faster than Brooks' fastest Vanwall. Indeed, Schell's BRM was the fastest green car, splitting Collins from Hawthorn and Musso. The Vanwalls were short of revs and a couple of engines were overheating. Moss was sixth fastest, a shade slower than Brooks. Further back, von Trips drove the fourth Ferrari, BRM ran a third car for Trintignant and Climax cars came from Cooper and Lotus as usual while Fangio made a surprise re-appearance in a revised 'Piccolo' Maserati 250F. In spite of withdrawal of its budget, the Modena factory team had refused to lie down and die!

Schell and Brooks beat Hawthorn from the grid but Hawthorn led at the end of the first lap with Schell, Musso, Moss, Brooks, Fangio, Collins, Behra and Lewis-Evans filling the first nine positions. Over the next couple of laps Musso and Collins came through to second and third positions while Schell fell back and Behra moved up, the BRMs running behind Brooks and Fangio while the other Vanwalls led the mid field men. On the fourth lap Collins took to an escape road, elevating Brooks to third. On the tenth of 50 laps Moss suddenly moved up, overtaking the BRMs and Fangio's 250F to run behind Brooks.

Tragically, Musso crashed on the next lap, suffering fatal injuries. On the following lap Brooks pitted with engine trouble and Fangio repassed Moss to run second. Von Trips and Trintignant also moved into the reckoning, the order Hawthorn, Fangio, Moss, Behra, von Trips, Schell, Trintignant, Lewis-Evans. Hawthorn was clear of the pack but Fangio, Moss and Behra were close and Behra suddenly leapfrogged to second. Fangio then slowed with clutch trouble, elevating von Trips to fourth.

Brooks had now taken over the Lewis-Evans car and was thus running well down the order. Trintignant retired and Schell made a long pit stop but Behra continued BRM's strong showing, duelling with Moss while von Trips held a lonely fourth. Gearbox failure saw Brooks post Vanwall's second retirement, then at the end of lap 40 Behra retired. Meanwhile, Collins was recovering and he overtook Fangio - now with brake trouble - for fourth, only to run out of fuel on the last lap. Thus, Moss finished second sandwiched by the Ferraris of Hawthorn a[nd] von Trips and Fangio finished fourt[h] resolved to make his retirement perm[a]nent.

Silverstone (GB) July 19
British Grand Prix
Moss .... *Q: 1/R:NR*
Brooks .... *Q: 9/R:7*
Lewis-Evans ..... *Q: 7/R:4*

Ferrari sent cars to England for Ha[w]thorn, Collins and von Trips and Ha[w]thorn was again on the front row. Ho[w]ever, three home built machines we[re] faster, Schell and Salvadori on the he[els] of Moss. The speed of the little Cooper w[as] a revelation on this plus-100 m.p.h. ave[r]age speed circuit. Salvadori was back[ed] by Brabham and Trintignant while Sch[ell] was backed by Behra, two cars from Lot[us] making a total of 13 works cars of whi[ch] only Moss and Schell broke the 100 se[c]ond barrier, Salvadori recording exact[ly] 100 seconds. Fifth on the grid, Alliso[n's] Climax-Lotus clocked an impressive 10[0] second lap, a full second quicker than t[he] two other Vanwalls.

Moss made the best start but from t[he] second row Collins soon passed him wh[ile] Hawthorn slotted into third ahead of Sch[ell], Brooks - up from the third row - Salvad[ori] and Lewis-Evans. Collins pulled aw[ay] from Moss who in turn pulled away fr[om] Hawthorn. Schell and Brooks then fad[ed] and Lewis-Evans got ahead of Salvad[ori] so that Ferrari and Vanwall filled the fi[rst] four positions. However, after 25 of [the] laps Salvadori got ahead of Lewis-Eva[ns], then Moss' engine failed.

Lewis-Evans could not reply to t[he] Cooper and Brooks was floundering [in] mid field and was lapped around h[alf] distance. Ferrari was left with a one-t[wo] result, runner up Hawthorn taking a[n]other fastest lap. Lewis-Evans finish[ed] fourth, hard on the heels of the remar[k]able Salvadori while Brooks remain[ed]

Diary continues on page 86

Furthermore, it caused all sorts of problems for the team engineers, particularly since they remained faithful to fuel injection. Avgas is far more sensitive to mixture strength than alcohol and it took an awful lot of development work to keep the Bosch system functional. For example, it was found that a greater fuel delivery was required at three quarter throttle than at full throttle.

This apparent anomaly is perhaps explained by the Vanwall engines' exploitation of inlet tract pressure waves. In view of this volumetric efficiency was considerably enhanced within a certain speed range which lay well below the peak power speed. Aside from injection system modification, the engine was given a revised exhaust system, pipes 1 and 4 and pipes 2 and 3 being mated to take the maximum advantage of exhaust tract pressure waves. The net result was elimination of previous flat spots in the power curve for a more driveable engine.

On the other hand, the loss of cooling through vaporisation of alcohol within the combustion chamber was a major worry, not least in terms

ss at Mirabeau, nte Carlo in '58. was only eighth on grid but took the from Hawthorn's 'ari on lap 32. s, half a dozen later the short- d Vanwall failed , a tappet king.

Diary continued

one lap down.

Nurburgring (D) August 3
German Grand Prix
Moss .... *Q: 3/NR*
Brooks .... *Q: 2/1*

Hawthorn pulled another superb lap out of the bag to take pole for the German Grand Prix, his third pole from four races. Brooks and Moss were hard on his heels, though, and the only other cars under 560 seconds. Due to a lack of engines Vanwall ran only two cars. Collins took the outside of the front row, then came von Trips, the Coopers of Salvadori and Trintignant ahead of the BRMs of Schell and Behra. Aside from Allison's Lotus and a couple of private Maseratis the rest of the field comprised a Formula Two division.

Brooks made the best start but Moss led the first lap with Hawthorn and Collins ahead of the second Vanwall and von Trips ahead of Schell who had likewise lost the advantage of a quick start. Trips ran into gearbox trouble on the second lap while Moss pulled steadily away from his pursuers. Lap three Moss ran at record speed, almost five seconds under Hawthorn's pole time while Collins overtook Hawthorn. Lap four Moss failed to complete. The Vanwall coasted to a halt at the Schwalbenschwanz, its ignition system lifeless.

That left Hawthorn leading back ahead of Collins and shadowed by Brooks, who was worried by a mid range misfire. Fourth was now Allison's little Lotus. The red cars continued to trade the lead; Brooks was speeded up by his pit and, throwing caution to the wind, on lap eight he caught them. Over the next couple of laps he took the lead through superior speed in the twists - aided by his disc brakes - only for superior engine power to tell on the long straight back to the pits. However, with his car misfiring only in mid range, Brooks could slipstream one or other of the Ferraris and then he had the advantage through the North and South curves, each lap managing to lead into the woods where he had the edge.

Alas, on lap 11 of 15, striving not to lose touch with the Vanwall Collins crashed at Pflanzgarten, sustaining serious injuries. His brake pedal is thought to have gone away. Hawthorn then retired with clutch trouble and Brooks ran home an easy winner from the Coopers of Salvadori and Trintignant, which profited from the demise of Allison's Lotus and were a third of a lap adrift of the cruising Vanwall. Moss had the consolation of fastest lap. There could be no compensation for the loss soon afterwards of that popular driver Peter Collins.

Oporto (POR) August 24
Portuguese Grand Prix
Moss .... *Q: 1/R:1*
Brooks .... *Q: 5/R:NR*
Lewis-Evans ..... *Q: 3/R:3*

The World Championship made its first visit to Portugal with three Vanwalls as usual and just two Ferraris, for Hawthorn and von Trips, the latter having a chassis with coil spring rear suspension. BRM, Cooper and Lotus were represented once again in a small field and Behra split Brooks from Lewis-Evans while Hawthorn in turn split Lewis-Evans from pole sitter Moss. Brabham was sixth quickest but was over three seconds from the 107m.p.h. pole time on the new anti clockwise 4.6 mile street circuit with its tram lines and cobblestones.

Moss made the best start to lead Hawthorn, Behra, Lewis-Evans, Brooks and Schell. Von Trips charged through to third on the first lap while Behra and Brooks fell back behind Schell and Lewis-Evans. Hawthorn overtook Moss on the second lap and Schell moved up to third, only to fall back behind von Trips, Beh[ra] and Lewis-Evans. Meanwhile, Moss sha[d]owed Hawthorn and Brooks fell furth[er] back, dropping as low as tenth befo[re] apparently coming to grips with the ci[r]cuit and speeding up.

On lap eight Moss took the lead onc[e] more and started to pull away. Behin[d] him Hawthorn led Behra and von Trip[s] with Lewis-Evans fifth until lap 15 o[n] which he demoted the Ferrari. Mea[n]while, Brooks was moving through th[e] mid field. Around two thirds distanc[e] Moss lapped Lewis-Evans and Hawthor[n] stopped for oil, after which he broke th[e] lap record in the process of chasing Behr[a]. Moss needed the point for fastest lap b[ut] misunderstood his pit signal and did n[ot] respond, believing he had it in the ba[g]. Meanwhile Brooks had come up to fift[h] behind Lewis-Evans and at that stage h[e] spun away his chances.

Hawthorn eventually caught Behra the[n] Moss lapped the BRM, bringing Lewis-Evans through to third in his slipstrea[m]. Thus, only Moss and Hawthorn com[]pleted the full race distance, the latte[r] finishing with faded brakes.

Monza (I) September 7
Italian Grand Prix
Moss .... *Q: 1/R:NR*
Brooks .... *Q: 2/R:1*
Lewis-Evans ..... *Q: 4/R:NR*

Ferrari's quest for a home win was bo[l]stered by the addition of Phil Hill an[d] Olivier Gendebien to its line up whil[e] Vanwall, BRM, Cooper and Lotus fle[w] the green. Both Vanwall and BRM ra[n] three cars - Joakim Bonnier in the thir[d] BRM - while Rob Walker ran a thir[d] Cooper for Trintignant. As in '57 th[e] banking was not used. Moss was again o[n] pole, with Brooks almost a second slowe[r] Hawthorn one-point-three seconds slow[er] again and Lewis-Evans a further secon[d] adrift on the outside of the front row. Th

Diary continues on page 88

rt of the Belgian
ınd Prix at Fran-
hamps, the field-
pouring into Eau
ıge led by Moss'
ıwall. Brooks is
d on his heels, then
es Gendebien's
ow Ferrari chased
the BRMs of
ra and Schell, the
raris of Collins
Hawthorn, the
rly placed Lewis-
ns Vanwall and
rest of the pack.
ss blew his
nces; Brooks won.

Diary continued

other Ferraris monopolised the second row, ahead of the three BRMs. Half a dozen private Maseratis added red to the lower half of the grid. Following Ferrari's evident disadvantage in Germany and Portugal, Hawthorn's Ferrari had disc brakes fitted while stronger Dino V6 engines were in all the Maranello cars.

Lewis-Evans was first off the grid but Phil Hill made an excellent start and was in the lead by the Ascari curve. The order at the end of the first lap was Hill, Moss, Lewis-Evans, Hawthorn, Brooks and Behra while a collision had eliminated Schell and von Trips and Gendebien had stalled at the start. Soon Hawthorn was up with Hill then on lap five he moved into the lead as the three Vanwalls gave chase. Then on lap seven Moss moved into the lead, after which Hill pitted with a thrown tread. Nevertheless, Hawthorn kept the pressure on, trading the lead with Moss.

While Hawthorn and Moss traded the lead, Brooks and Behra traded fourth place but after 13 of 70 laps Brooks suffered a broken c.v. boot, the car pitting belching oil smoke. Behra then challenged Lewis-Evans and on lap 16 went ahead of Moss, only to drop back behind the two Vanwalls. On lap 18 Moss went missing, a shaft in his gearbox having seized.

Behra remained in the picture until the 29th lap when he struck brake problems, leaving Hawthorn worried by only Lewis-Evans. Alas, the Vanwall retired after 31 laps with overheating. After 35 laps Hawthorn made a stop for tyres and all the while Brooks was regaining ground, as was Hill. As Hawthorn pitted, Hill had a couple of laps in the lead then he too required fresh tyres. Masten Gregory's private 250F then lay second to Hawthorn and Brooks steadily reeled it in. After 47 laps the Maserati was another to stop for tyres, this elevating Brooks to second.

Brooks had the choice of stopping for fresh tyres or gambling and going for the win. Suffering clutch slip, Hawthorn was now less than ten seconds ahead of the Vanwall. Brooks decided against stopping and steadily caught the Ferrari, passing it with ten laps to run. Keeping a careful eye on his hard worked left rear he ran home the clear winner. Hill finished third - team orders keeping him behind Hawthorn, though he had fastest lap to his credit.

Casablanca (MOR) October 19

Moroccan Grand Prix
Moss .... *Q: 2/R:1*
Brooks .... *Q: 7/R:NR*
Lewis-Evans ..... *Q: 3/R:NR*

The title chase was now a cliffhanger: Moss could succeed if he won and set fastest lap, but only with Hawthorn lower than second. In practice Moss had to take second to Hawthorn, by a mere tenth of a second. Lewis-Evans and Behra were next up, the BRM driver once again setting a commendable time and having been fastest the first day. BRM ran a total of four cars, adding Flockhart to its line up. Ferrari ran three cars, Gendebien's coil sprung car joining Hawthorn in the use of disc brakes while Phil Hill drove the third entry. Cooper again was represented by three cars, Jack Fairman replacing Brabham while Lotus had its usual brace of Climax cars.

Moss rocketed into the lead from the middle of the front row with Hill hard on his tail, then Bonnier and Hawthorn ahead of Brooks and Lewis-Evans. Hill pushed Moss hard for three laps, only to have to take to an escape road as he over-optimistically attempted to outbrake the disc-braked Vanwall. Meanwhile Hawthorn had run third ahead of Bonnier, behind whom Hill rejoined. Hill soon overtook Bonnier and Hawthorn let him through so that he might continue to harass Moss. However, Moss proved able to hold hi margin over the young Ferrari driver.

Further back Bonnier was overtake by Brooks who put the pressure o Hawthorn while, hampered by a sic engine, Lewis-Evans slipped back behin Gendebien and Behra. Brooks set a ne lap record as he pressured Hawthorn an after 19 laps he moved into third. Eigh laps later Hawthorn got back in front o the Vanwall and soon afterwards the gree car blew its engine, throwing oil onto th rear tyres which sent it spinning into th desert. Gendebien then spun off on th oil.

With Bonnier dropping back the BRM had not featured and now Behra joine Flockhart in retirement. However, Bon nier was still ahead of Lewis-Evans. Mos put in the fastest lap to ensure the maxi mum possible points score but Ferrari were still second and third with Bonnie protecting Hawthorn from the secon Vanwall. With ten laps to go Lewis-Evans engine blew and the car spun off the roa and broke a fuel line which caused a fire Lewis-Evans received burns. Moss wen on to win but predictably Hill slowed t allow Hawthorn to take second and th World Championship.

Nevertheless, Vanwall had won th new Manufacturers' Championship. Ala 58 year old Tony Vandervell's Triump was marred a few days later as Lewis Evans succumbed to his injuries.

ening lap of the ·ch Grand Prix at ·dvoort - again ·ss leads. This ·e Lewis-Evans is ·nd and he is fol- ·ed by Schell's ·M, Brooks, the ·rprisingly fleet ·e Cooper of ·bham, Behra's ·M and the rest.

of soaring exhaust valve temperatures. On the mandatory 108/135 octane Avgas the compression ratio fell to 11.5:1 and valve timing as well as the combustion chamber shape had to be modified. The power loss was reportedly 17b.h.p. at the top end and 6b.h.p. in the mid range. In view of the increased thermal loading sodium cooled inlet valves were employed and an oil spray was directed onto the underside of the piston. Nevertheless, the engine failures of '58 that afflicted Moss at Monte Carlo and Silverstone, Lewis-Evans at Monte Carlo (via the header tank thence to the steering), Zandvoort, Rheims and Monza and Brooks at Casablanca are understandable.

Those eight retirements should be seen in the context of a total of 15 retirements from 26 starts, including one accident. The other six mechanical failures were down to a plug, the ignition, the rear axle, the throttle and - twice - to the gearbox. Further, a lack of engines saw only two Vanwalls run at the 'Ring. Overall, although Hawthorn was wonderfully consistent, the reliability of the Ferrari V6 was not markedly

The 1958 Av
burning versio
the V254 en
produced in
region of 2
270b.h.p. whe
over 300b.h.p.
possible g
unrestricted f
The transitio
Avgas was a head
for the injec
technicians due
its greater sensiti
to mixture stren

...s collects second ...e at Rheims in ...8. He simply ...d not catch the ...ari of arch-rival ...thorn. This sea... the Ferrari had more powerful en... and its aerody...ics were im...ed, Maranello ...rly inspired by ...in's work for ...wall.

better: such is often the nature of Grand Prix racing.

Ferrari continued to suffer a tyre disadvantage with its continuing dependency upon Engelbert rubber. Dunlop had not enjoyed a better reputation previously but by 1958 important change was afoot at the Birmingham company's base. Dunlop had been involved in International racing for a decade, first with its R1 tubed crossply tyre that had a conventional cotton carcase and a natural rubber tread. Its domed crown carried a tread around three inches wide and its aspect ratio - the ratio of its section height (measured from bead level to the top of the crown) to section width (measured between bulging sidewalls) was around 100%.

In 1955 Dunlop introduced the R3 (R2 having been dropped at the development stage) this similar tyre bringing a carbon black rather than zinc oxide (white) based compound for carcase reinforcement. Whereas white casings had been limited to a maximum running temperature around 85 degrees, a black casing could tolerate up to 95 degrees. The R3 was soon accompanied by the R4 developed specifically for wet weather use. However, these tyres were not employed by the majority of Grand Prix front runners in the remaining free fuel days.

Meanwhile, Dunlop was developing a revolutionary nylon ply carcase - as sampled by Vanwall in '57 - and for 1958 it furnished Vanwall with development versions of the R3 based around

this new technology. The nylon ply carcase offered greater flexibility with greater tensile strength. The flexibility allowed the tyre to conform to the road better, increasing the effective footprint area by as much as 10%, while the strength allowed a thinner, cooler running casing with more even heat distribution.

The net result, if used properly was improved grip, while a potentially lower inflation pressure could (in theory) enhance adhesion on bumpy surfaces. With the nylon carcase there was more room to adjust inflation pressure in accordance with driver preference and car suspension requirements. With the cotton carcase a pressure in the region of 50p.s.i. had been necessary - now significantly lower pressures could be safely run.

Together with its switch to Dunlop tyres the Vanwall suspension had been modified with a thinner front anti roll bar while at the 'Ring Brooks car had the negative camber removed from the rear wheels. This gave him earlier breakaway, which he preferred to counteract the inherent understeer of the car. Understeer was promoted by running wire spoke wheels at the front, more rigid alloy disc wheels at the rear but this combination enhanced brake cooling. After Monaco - where the new alloy wheels were run front and rear - wire front wheels were regular wear. Brooks preferred discs at both ends.

At Morocco the team introduced a lightweight hub for the wire wheel since tyre changes had become a thing of the past. Another modification was the earlier introduction of telescopic steering dampers, in time for the French Grand Prix, following the experience of wheel tremor at Francorchamps.

It had been suspected that the car might require additional radiator area with the switch to Avgas but this did not prove to be the case. At Oporto the Vanwalls appeared with the oil cooler atop the water radiator rather than riding on its back and ram-fed via a nose scoop, this to combat the Portugese summer heat. The effect was to lower the water temperature by around 30 degrees while the oil ran slightly hotter.

The relocated cooler stayed on for Monza (the cars were shipped direct) and in practice Moss tried a bubble cockpit canopy of blown perspex devised by Costin. Since it was blown there was no distortion but a small hole was cut to allow Moss to check for oil on the track. The canopy gave him an additional 50 revs while causing a slight feeling of insecurity. Of greater concern to Moss was the noise within the canopy, which was unbearable, even wearing ear plugs. For that reason it was rejected.

In spite of the significant cut in power, the Vanwall went faster in 1958 than it had done in 1957. This is perhaps partly explained by the improved engine driveability but far more significant was the new tyre technology. The nylon ply carcase R3 worked extremely well on the softly sprung Vanwall chassis and grip was enhanced. Further, the new tyre wore extremely well. At Monza all the Ferraris had to stop for fresh covers but Brooks ran through non-stop to victory, keeping a wary eye on the left rear since that took the greatest pounding.

Thus, the new nylon ply carcase tyre was a key factor in the Vanwall success of 1958. As we have noted, Ferrari continued with unsatisfactory Engelbert tyres - and only late in the season did it switch to disc brakes. Collins had Dunlop discs fitted to his 250GT road car and that equipment was transferred to Hawthorn's racer, following the tragedy at the 'Ring. The improvement was immediately apparent.

The Ferrari V6 was a device derived from Formula Two, a category which had switched to hydrocarbon fuel earlier. The new Dino engine took its name from Ferrari's late son who had assisted Vittorio Jano (creator of the D.50) in its design. First seen in a combined Formula One and Two race at Naples in '57, the original 1500cc. Dino V6 (70 x 64.5mm.) had been specifically designed to run on pump petrol.

The Dino V6 boasted twin overhead camshafts, and two valves per cylinder opened by mushroom tappets and closed by coil springs rather than Maranello's traditional hairpin variety. The valves were set at 60 degrees included in a typical hemi head. Twin ignition was em-

Previous spre Moss at Silverst looking for suc on home territ He qualified on but Collins overt on the first lap sadly the Vanw soon failed him. H the Ace makes the oversteer like the Maserati 25 though the natu tendency of the gr machine was to c fortable underst

Costin devised bubble canopy for at Monza and it g Moss an additio 50r.p.m. Howe noise was so unbe able within, it ha be abandon

ployed, along with Weber carburettors in the valley of the vee, these feeding through beneficially straight downdraught ports.

Jano's chain driven, light alloy unit ran to 9,000r.p.m. producing 180b.h.p. The Avgas burning 2.5 litre version developed for 1958 displaced 85 x 71.0mm. for 2417cc. and produced a claimed 280b.h.p. at 8,500r.p.m. Ferrari - drawing on the acknowledged genius of Jano - had thus successfully risen to the challenge of replacing chemical weaponry by mechanical ingenuity. However, the slower running Vanwall four was comfortably ahead in terms of power per litre per 1000r.p.m.

The challenge of the Prancing Horse was let down by inferior cornering and braking performance. Its chassis technology was similar to that seen in '57 and was not good enough to exploit the Maranello power advantage to full effect. For example, at Francorchamps Vanwall could get through the Masta Kink faster than Ferrari, and had superior aerodynamics to help overcome its power disadvantage. Mind you, this year the Ferrari was more slippery than in years past as was evidenced by the speed at Rheims.

Thus, overall the red and green cars were closely matched with Vanwall generally having an edge thanks to the genius of Moss, the benefit of Dunlop's new technology, the careful three-year honing of its well thought out chassis, the overall integration of its team and the sheer

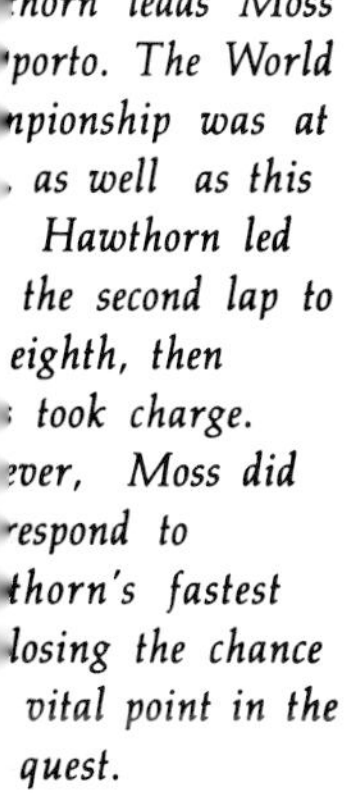

thorn leads Moss porto. The World npionship was at as well as this Hawthorn led the second lap to eighth, then took charge. ever, Moss did respond to thorn's fastest losing the chance vital point in the quest.

determination underlying G.A. Vandervell's crusade.

Old rival BRM had produced an even smaller, even lighter car in line with the switch to shorter races and lighter fuel loads. The chassis handled well and Behra and Schell strengthened the Bourne World Championship bid. On Avgas BRM claimed an impressive 270b.h.p. The net result was shared fastest qualifying time at Monte Carlo for Behra, and the lead for 27 laps before a brake system failure intervened. At Zandvoort Schell and Behra were a good second and third to Moss then the marque lost speed at Francorchamps, this later traced to a serious shortage of steam.

The team bounced back with third on the grid for Schell at Rheims, second at Silverstone but neither challenge was sustained on race day. BRM did not live up to its early season promise. At the 'Ring handling was awry, at Oporto the team was again overshadowed by Vanwall and Ferrari. Behra got into the thick of the fight at Monza, only to suffer brake failure, then at Casablanca even an entry of four cars could not upset the Vanwall - Ferrari duel. Overall, an inconclusive season as poor relation to the London team carrying the Green out front.

So many seasons had passed since Guy Anthony Vandervell had been a leading patron of BRM and finally he had succeeded where BRM had failed. However, times were changing fast and he was not getting any younger. Almost 60 years old, he still ruled a vast business empire as well as an exceptional racing team. The strain was enormous: his doctor prescribed a complete rest as the only way to avoid a nervous breakdown.

Vandervell had left BRM taking the view that to get a job done properly you need to do it yourself. Rightly or wrongly, he had always striven to do it all himself, both in commerce and in racing. Now the effort of overthrowing the red had all but broken his health and the loss of Lewis-Evans had dampened his enthusiasm. With regret he released his loyal team members to find other positions in the clamour of the Grand Prix pit lane, leaving him at Park Royal with his cars, his memories and in the racing 'shop, the dignified silence of an important museum.